ADDISON WESLEY LONGMAN HISTORY IN DEPTH SERIES

KT-493-585

# HITLER AND NAZISM 1933–45

Jane Jenkins
Series editor: Christopher Culpin

| NORWICH CITY COLLEGE LIBRARY | | | |
|---|---|---|---|
| Stock No. | 203110 | | |
| Class | 947·086 JEN | | |
| Cat. | | Proc. | |

# CONTENTS

# PART ONE

# INTRODUCTION

The future leader of the Third Reich was appointed Chancellor of Germany on 30 January 1933. This was at a time when, according to many contemporaries, Hitler was no longer seen as a problem and his movement (the National Socialists) had ceased to be a political danger. This was based on election results; for in the elections, on 6 November 1932, his Nazi Party had polled 33.1 per cent of the vote, giving it 196 seats out of a total of 584. This result represented a drop in the Party's performance from the previous election of 31 July 1932, when it had polled 37.4 per cent, with 230 out of 608 seats. Nevertheless, although he had failed to secure a majority, Hitler was still the leader of the largest political party in parliament.

**In your initial survey of the events in this chapter think about the following lines of enquiry:**

- **What was the link, if any, between Hitler's appointment in January 1933 and the state of Germany?**
- **Did Hitler matter? Was he pivotal to the State?**
- **Was Nazism revolutionary?**
- **Were the fears of some contemporaries that Hitler would bring ruin to Germany justified?**
- **Was January 1933 a decisive date in world history?**

## Domestic and foreign events

**1933** Hitler secures his one-party state

**1934** 'Night of the Long Knives'
Death of President Hindenburg; Hitler becomes Führer

**1935** Saar returned to Germany
Compulsory military service introduced
Stresa Front of Italy, France and Britain against Germany
Anglo-German Naval Agreement is signed
Nuremberg Laws – discriminated against the Jews

**1936** Hitler re-occupies the Rhineland illegally
Hitler recognises full sovereignty of Austria
Four Year Plan to make the economy self-sufficient in preparation for a war
Rome–Berlin Axis
Anti-Comintern Pact between Germany and Japan is directed against Russia

**1937** Secret directive of War Minister Werner von Blomberg indicates Czechoslovakia as a possible target

**1938** Hitler becomes supreme commander of the Wehrmacht
*Anschluss* (union of Austria with Germany)
Hitler seizes Sudetenland (Czechoslovakia)
*Kristallnacht* ('Crystal Night') – destruction of Jewish property

**1939** German troops march into the rest of Czechoslovakia
Hitler demands the return of Danzig and the Polish Corridor from Poland
Germany annexes the Memel territory in Lithuania
Pact of Steel between Germany and Italy
Russo-German Non-Aggression Pact is signed
Hitler invades Poland. Britain and France at war with Germany
Russian troops occupy East Poland
Heydrich presents his plans for ghettos in Poland
Attempted assassination of Hitler at a beer cellar in Munich

**1940** First deportation of Jews begins to German-occupied Poland
German invasion of Denmark and Norway, Netherlands, Belgium, Luxembourg and France
'Madagascar Plan' – transportation of 4 million Jews from West Europe
Warsaw ghetto sealed

**1941** German invasion of Yugoslavia, Greece and Russia
Göring orders Heydrich to embark on the 'Final Solution'
Transport of Jews to the camps begins
Germany declares war on the USA

**1942** Conference at Wannsee agrees to final details of the Holocaust
First mass killings of Jews marks the beginning of 'Aktion Reinhard'
The Reichstag grants Hitler full authority in executive, legislative and judicial functions
Jews deported to the East
German defeat at El Alamein – allied landings in North Africa
The 'Brunner action' in Berlin and the intensification of mass deportations

**1943** German declaration of Total War
German surrender in North Africa
Allied landings in Sicily and overthrow of Mussolini

**1944** First V-1 missiles fired on Britain
Allied landings in Normandy

Bomb Plot against Hitler in his East Prussian HQ
Goebbels given powers to mobilise for total war
First V-2 bombers launched to bomb London
Himmler orders the suspension of the liquidation of Jews and those under arrest are to be used for the 'total war effort'

**1945** Liberation of Auschwitz by Soviet troops
Hitler's 'Nero Order' to destroy all industrial plant
Battle for Berlin begins – falls to the Red Army
Himmler offers to surrender to the Allies
Hitler's last will and testament recognises Admiral Dönitz as his successor
Hitler commits suicide in Berlin bunker
Germany surrenders in the US HQ in Rheims and Soviet HQ in Berlin
Allied Control Commission assumes control and the NSDAP is abolished.

# Germany in 1933

## Political system in 1933

Germany's political system in 1933 was democratic and federal. It had been introduced following the abdication of its monarch and as a preliminary to the negotiations which led to the 1919 Versailles peace settlement. The latter had dismantled the German Empire in the wake of defeat in the First World War. However, although the Kaiser abdicated in 1918 this was not followed by the removal of the remaining elites. They continued to dominate the bureaucracy and civil service. Unfortunately, they lacked not only the training to manage a democratic system of government, but also the motivation and commitment. The legend grew that Germany had been 'stabbed in the back' and this had a powerful impact on many Germans after 1918.

The Constitution was based on an attempt to replicate the democratic constitutions of Britain and the United States. It was called the Weimar Republic after the town where those who drew up the Constitution met. It consisted of:

**1 Parliament**

This was composed of two houses:

- The **Reichstag** was the lower house and the most important part of the Constitution. It was elected by universal suffrage on a system of proportional representation (*i.e.* parties were given seats in accordance with the proportion of votes cast for them). Ministers were responsible to it. This system of election encouraged multiple parties which remained the bane of the Weimar Republic.

- The **Reichstat** was the upper house representing the different states (called 'Lander') of Germany. Its powers were limited to delaying legislation which had already been passed by the Reichstag.

### 2 Chancellor

The German Chancellor was similar to a British prime minister. He made policy decisions. He was appointed by the President and had a place in the Reichstag.

### 3 President

The President was head of state and elected by universal suffrage for a period of seven years. His most important right, under Article 48 of the Weimar Constitution, was to rule by presidential decree and without consultation if the Reichstag was unable to produce a decisive majority on an issue. This gave him the power to suspend civil liberties in an emergency. Paul Hindenburg had held this office since 1925.

The problem for Germany was that this constitution was introduced into a country whose politicians had no experience of a parliamentary system. They were divided in political opinion and unaccustomed to the 'give and take' of consensus democratic politics. People found it difficult to transfer their loyalty from a royal figure standing above party and give it to a president.

In the view of historians, Germany's republican government came to an end before the Nazis took over, though they contributed to its collapse. The Constitution had started to break down from 1930. This was due to the impact of recurring political crises arising from an inability of successive governments to deal with the collapse of the German economy. The Reichstag was torn apart by warring political groups and extremists so that ministers ruled without a parliament. When Hitler became Chancellor, the President ruled using his decree-making powers under Article 48 to deal with a wide range of matters.

On his appointment as Chancellor, Hitler was expected to govern by this system. There was no suggestion that a new system of government – the Third Reich – would be introduced. Those who had helped Hitler

**Figure 1** Germany's territorial ambitions and acquisitions

come to power, particularly the conservative aristocrat Franz von Papen, intended that he should be little more than a figurehead in a cabinet still dominated by conservative nationalists of the German National People's Party (the DNVP). In fact, Hitler was one of only three Nazis in a cabinet of 12. The others were Wilhelm Frick (Minister of the Interior) and Hermann Göring (Minister for Prussia, the largest and most important state in the federal republic).

### Source

*I have got Hindenburg's confidence. In two months' time we will have squeezed Hitler into a corner until he squeaks.*

*Von Papen writing to a friend soon after Hitler's appointment, quoted in H. W. Koch (ed.)* ***Aspects of the Third Republic*** *(Macmillan, 1985)*

Von Papen's confidence was not shared by all. Subsequent events were to confirm their fears. Hitler's appointment was one of the most significant events of the twentieth century. It soon became apparent that, under cover of legality, a revolution was carried out by Hitler and his violent mass movement which transformed Germany into a one-party dictatorship bent on challenging, in the longer run, the existing international order. Therefore 30 January 1933 is a decisive date in world history. It led to the establishment of the Nazi dictatorship and to the Second World War, with all its far-reaching consequences.

## Nature of German society in 1933

German society was relatively poor in European terms as a result of the immediate impact of the 1929 depression whose effects Germany had felt more strongly than either Britain or France. Even so, its underlying economic base was strong, hence the rapid recovery it was to experience under the Nazi regime. However, in 1933 it was experiencing all the effects of a 'social catastrophe'. Recent research has tried to stress the relationship between the National Socialist German Workers' Party (NSDAP) and this sense of crisis and demoralisation. Many Germans viewed Hitler as 'a truly charismatic leader' whom they 'followed blindly, as if he possessed a divine judgement, for the next 12 tempestuous years'.

In 1933 German society was still dominated by the old imperial attitudes and privileges. The Kaiser's abdication and exile in 1917 had not been accompanied by a bloodbath so that an autocratic elite continued to enjoy their privileges of political power.

## The elites

- **Junkers** were the rich, landowning class in Germany, descended from the former militaristic Prussian nobility. They took the style 'Von' to indicate their status. Their power-base was in large estates along the North German plain and east of the river Elbe. Over one-sixth of Germany's total arable area was owned by 17,070 Junkers and middle-class owners. They were conservative and nationalist and bitterly opposed to any suggestion of Communism. They were represented in politics by the conservative German National People's Party (DNVP).
- The **industrialists** were the owners of large industry in the Ruhr basin, North Rhine, Westphalia and the Saar. They included such families as the Krupps, Loewe, Wolf and Mercedes-Benz. They too were conservative and nationalist and were also represented in politics by the DNVP.
- The **'old bureaucracy'** held high administrative posts in the Civil Service, judiciary and services. They believed they owed service to the State and not to the Weimar Republic. They were still intent on trying to exercise unrestricted power which they considered more important than 'liberty'. They were anti-republican in attitude and hoped for the return of monarchy.

The elites had grown up and risen in their careers in a period when military values dominated. Before 1914 they had contributed to Germany's readiness to enter a major European war. The elites looked for economic policies to protect their interests against peasants and workers. This meant that they looked for wage reductions, a fall in social welfare payments and for a fall in state interference in the economy.

## Farmers/peasants

Germany was a society of village dwellers. Those who gained their livelihood from agriculture formed 25 per cent of the population. They were located along the North German plain and east of the river Elbe. The size of their land-holding varied: the majority of peasants – some 60 per cent – were restricted to one-sixth of the land in holdings of less than 12 acres (under 5 hectares). The average income of peasants was 600 marks a year (compared with 1,000 marks for workers). The peasants were hard working and their lives centred on their village and home.

### The workers

These were the largest group, accounting for 46 per cent of the population. The 'working class' in Germany of the 1920s was an imprecise category. They ranged from those who worked in large factories or mines to small workshops or self-employed. Workers tended to be craft workers and thought of themselves as 'masters' or 'apprentices'.

### The middle class (who were called the *mittelstand*)

Below the elites, Germany was a country of small businesses and light manufacturing with large numbers of traditional craftworkers and small business/retail shops and cafes. Their situation was below the level of semi-skilled workers; they were disadvantaged by competition from cheap American goods during the 1920s. They were hit by widespread poverty across society and shared with the peasants and impoverished clerks the difficulties of the 1920s' economy. There was a reduction in the number of hours worked from 7.5 to 6 hours average a day so all those in employment had declining earnings. Small businesses found that their income was cut by 50 per cent between 1929 and 1932 – a catastrophe for owners who had nothing to fall back on.

Apart from the small-scale businessmen, the middle-class group also included those who were employed in providing services – such as doctors, lawyers, schoolteachers and those intellectuals who contributed to the cultural and artistic life of Germany.

In 1933 those who composed the *mittelstand* had became increasingly bitter since they felt their interest had been ignored by successive governments. As a consequence, they had deserted the political parties of the Right (namely the DNVP, DVP or DDP) or Catholic Centre (Zentrum) and had moved closer to the extreme Right (the NSDAP).

**Table 1** Distribution of the population by economic activity, June 1933

| Economic activity | % |
|---|---|
| Agriculture and forestry | 24.5 |
| Industry and handicrafts | 34.2 |
| Commerce and trade | 15.6 |
| Public service and the free professions | 7.1 |
| Domestic service | 3.3 |
| Self-employed without a profession | 15.3 |

Census of 16 June 1933 published by Reich Statistical Office; quoted in J. Noakes and G. Pridham (eds) *Nazism 1919–45, A Documentary Reader* Vol. II (1984)

### Support for Hitler and his Party

The Nazi Party aimed at national power by persuading people that their particular local grievance mattered at a national level – unlike other parties. Hitler built up and communicated with his 'constituency' (Germany) as a Messiah. He had enormous self-belief in his mission to seize national power and to stop decline. He made a conscious effort to convey to the German people a particular propaganda image of himself as 'our last hope'. People supported Hitler less because of Nazi ideology, but more because of the powerful manufacture of the Führer myth based on a view of Hitler as 'our last hope', 'a saviour', 'a redeemer'. From 1931 he had concentrated on this propaganda image of building a strong nation to cut across party. This message was difficult to sustain but the Nazi Party was successful in reconciling local politics with Hitler at the centre. Not everyone believed this – for only a third of the electorate voted NSDAP.

## Hitler and Nazism

Prior to becoming Chancellor in 1933, Hitler and his NSDAP put forward certain beliefs. These appeared to bring together the two opposed beliefs of 'nationalism' and 'socialism'. This would lead to difficulties. It created different expectations both from within his party and from his supporters. However, Nazi propaganda preferred to show Hitler leading a party that was 'on the move'. Goebbels aimed at a breadth of appeal across social groups. What were these beliefs? Try filling in the right-hand column in the table overleaf.

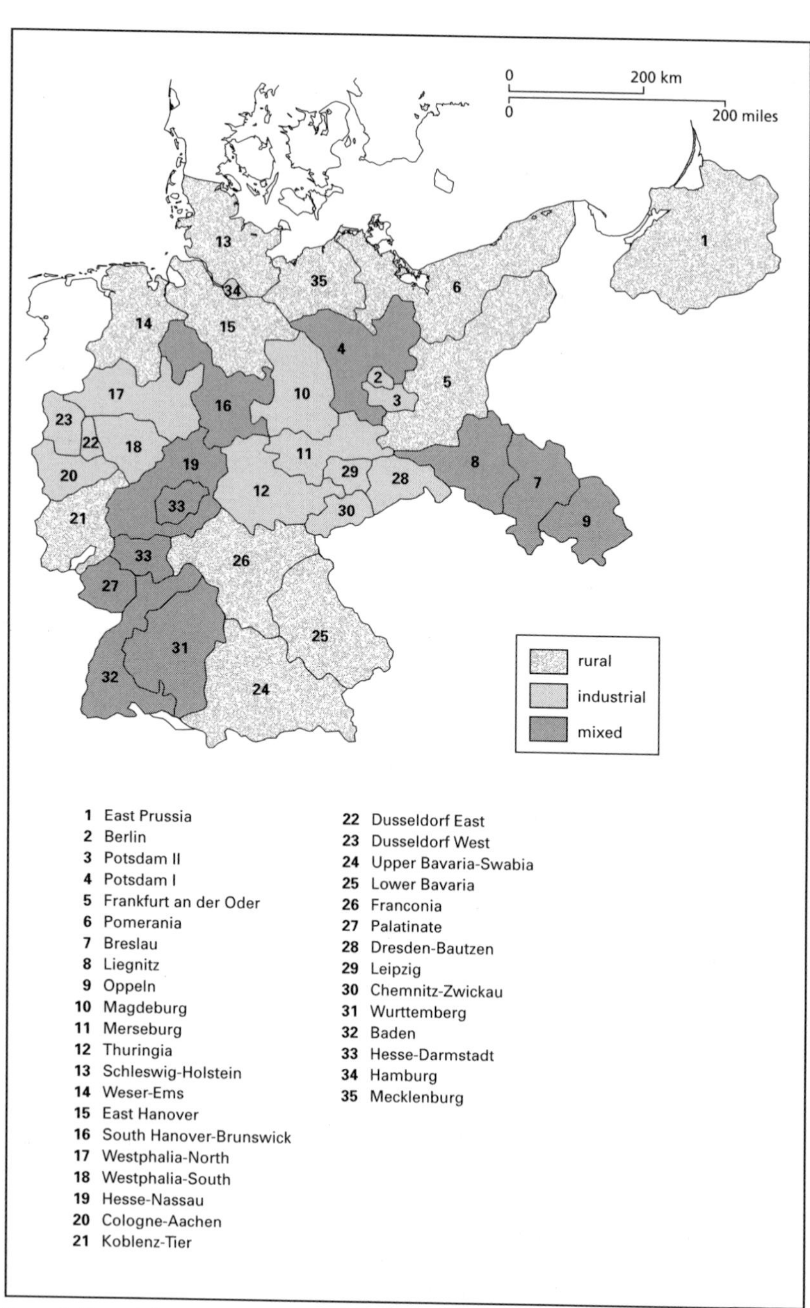


**Figure 2** Electoral districts of Germany in 1933 according to economic activity

| Belief | Who supported these ideas? |
|---|---|
| 1 Nationalism<br>• Union of all Germans into a 'Greater Reich' (which would also include the Sudeten Germans)<br>• Recovery of territory lost in the 1919 Treaty of Versailles<br>• Strong sense of community – the *völk* | |
| 2 Patriotism<br>• Restore national prestige. | |
| 3 Militarism<br>• Rearm to create a strong national army<br>• Expand German frontier to the East in the interests of more food/living space (*lebensraum*). | |
| 4 Anti-Semitism<br>• Need to remove Jews as a corrupting influence. No Jew to be a German citizen. | |
| 5 Racial purity<br>• Elimination of inferior stock including mentally and physically handicapped<br>• Superiority of the Aryan races – the master race (*Herrenvölk*). | |
| 6 Power of the State/Führer Principle<br>• Submissiveness of the individual<br>• Overthrow of parliamentary democracy/Weimar system of government<br>• Strong authoritarian government. | |
| 7 Socialism<br>• Abolition of all unearned income<br>• Profit sharing in industry<br>• Generous provision for the old<br>• Education of poor children at state expense. | |

# Chronological survey of the Third Reich

## Consolidation of power, January 1933–June 1934

The Nazi revolution followed Hitler becoming Chancellor on the 30 January 1933. The position of the Nazis at the end of January 1933 was that they were partners in a coalition government, but without a majority in the Reichstag. January 1933 to August 1934 saw the replacement of a democratic system by a one-party state. This consolidation of power went smoothly because:

- The Nazis had the money and the force to support their campaign. Hitler did not aim to destroy the State, but to take over State machinery and use it to make the 'revolution'. He used all the forms of the constitution and the legal system to establish his dictatorship legally. Much had already been achieved prior to 1933 because under the impact of the 1929 depression successive governments had relied on Article 48 to govern Germany under presidential decree.
- Terror was of vital importance. There is evidence that it came from grassroots level rather than being planned or even controlled by the leadership who often acted in response to this terror.
- Opposition and resistance in Germany disappeared in 1933 because Hitler's opponents on the Left were fatally divided.
- Considerable numbers supported the sweeping away of democracy.

Hitler wanted to secure a majority in the Reichstag. New elections were called for 5 March. The Nazi Party was presented as an alternative to the weak democratic system which had rested on the Socialist and the Catholic Centre parties. The other parties, Hitler argued, had failed in foreign policy and had brought economic ruin at home. Göring played a prominent part because, as Minister for Prussia, he controlled nearly two-thirds of Germany. He purged the Prussian civil service and police of officials opposed to the NSDAP and replaced them with Nazis. His main attack was against the Communists and took the form of skilful propaganda and sound tactics. On 27 February the Reichstag burnt down. The responsibility was laid against the

Communists although many believed the Nazis to be the culprits. As a result of the fire:

- Hitler issued the emergency 'Presidential decree for the Protection of the German People' which suspended the clauses of the Weimar Constitution guaranteeing personal liberty.
- Göring arrested leading Communist and Socialist politicians.

A high number of people (nearly 90 per cent) voted in the 5 March elections. The Nazis increased their vote by nearly 10 per cent more than they had secured in November 1932. With the absence of the Communists, the NSDAP had a majority in the Reichstag without requiring the support of the conservative National People's Party. Hitler had become independent of Von Papen and Hindenburg.

Hitler's next task was to make himself supreme by getting rid of those who might challenge his authority. Strengthened by his success, he secured the Enabling Law which gave him dictatorial powers to govern by decree. He then launched a policy of creating the National Socialist Constituency through the policy of coordination known as *Gleichschaltung*. This aimed at a complete unity of political, social and economic life with the application of terror as a deterrent. The Gestapo (secret state police) was developed by Göring during April–November 1933. No one who dared to oppose the regime would be spared. A series of measures removed all potential opposition through the:

- subordination of the state governments to Berlin through the appointment of governors (*Reichstathalter*). The traditional 'federal' Germany, with its many competing sovereignties, was replaced by a centralised German State;
- abolition of trade unions which were replaced by the German Labour Front (DAF);
- abolition of all other political parties;
- agreement with the Catholic Church;
- rapid takeover of the media and the educational system.

This political centralisation amounted to a revolution. But it would be wrong to suppose – as the Socialist and Communist critics did – that the Nazi regime was a dictatorship imposed by force on an unwilling people. Hitler carried through his policy of *Gleichschaltung* without opposition. He was surprised by the collapse of opposition from his more moderate opponents who could offer little resistance. Hitler then sought to reach an agreement with other powerful institutions in the state.

The challenge came from within the NSDAP which was divided by jealousies and fear. Hitler was pushed by the left wing of the Nazi Party led by Röhm and his supporters for a second social revolution to complete the political seizure. In July 1933 Hitler gave a warning to the extremists and the ***SA*** and declared that they had achieved the first three stages of revolution: preparation, seizure and a one-party state. Order was now required, not a second revolution. Others disagreed.

## KEY TERMS

The **SA (*Sturmabteilung*)** were the Nazi paramilitary corps. Initially formed to protect meetings and to disrupt those of opponents, the SA became a huge organisation of some 400,000 men by 1932, many of them recruited from the unemployed. Its relations with the NSDAP were sometimes troubled and Hitler had to quash several local revolts, including one in Berlin. It was the SA that became impatient and threatened violence when Hitler stuck to his tactics of legality in 1932. The Reichswehr needed the support of this large body of 'nationally' minded men and could not afford to incur its hostility. After 30 January 1933 the SA provided the terroristic element in the Nazi takeover, which accompanied Hitler's show of legality. Political opponents were tortured and killed in the secret bunkers of the SA and in 'wild' concentration camps.

The **SS (*Schutzstaffel*)** was a small formation charged with the protection of the Führer. It expanded in 1933 and, with the elimination of the SA as a major factor in June 1934, became one of the main empires within the Nazi state under Himmler.

Röhm and the SA wanted a 'second revolution'. This was a vague concept, but it included revolutionary changes in the economy and the ownership of industry, as well as the SA becoming Germany's new revolutionary national army.

Hitler was aware that he needed the support of the German Army (*Reichswehr*) to remain in power and to succeed to the Presidency. He could not afford disorder while his regime was still consolidating its hold on power. He responded to Röhm's demands by declaring that the revolutionary phase of the takeover was at an end in the autumn of 1933. The *Reichswehr* hated the radical socialist elements of the SA and was jealous of its larger organisation. It felt threatened by Röhm's plans.

Hitler was in a dilemma – the SA was useful to him as a blackmail and pressure on the *Reichswehr* and the right-wing forces of industry and finance, but Röhm challenged his authority and leadership. Matters came to a crisis in the summer of 1934. Hitler reached an understanding with the generals. The Army would remain the national source of power and the SA would be kept subordinate. The outcome of this was that on 30 June 1934 Hitler abandoned attempts at reconciliation. The 'Night of the Long Knives' was seen by Hitler as a justified purge of the SA whom he declared had been planning a *coup d'état* (see Figure 3 overleaf).

It was the biggest political murder in European history for centuries. Yet it was presented to the Germans as the suppression of dangerous radical elements and the victory of decency through the will of the Führer. The SA lost its importance, but the **SS** soon took its place as the most powerful and sinister empire within the Nazi state.

## Maintenance of power, 1934 onwards

On 2 August 1934, Hindenburg died. Hitler assumed the highest functions of the State, becoming President and Chancellor and taking the title of 'Führer'. The Nazi revolution was complete. However, Hitler still had some important restraints on his power: he had not yet gained control of the Army and the Churches, and he was still dependent on an alliance with the elites. Apart from these considerations, the supremacy of the Führer was applied in every sphere of party and state. He decided policy, made laws and controlled foreign policy. The key institutions of government lost much of their importance:

- The Cabinet was dominated by Hitler and other top Nazis and was used less as the central instrument of government.
- The Reichstag did not disappear but the political parties did. It became a Nazi assembly composed of select party men. It did not legislate, but only advised and approved Hitler's policies.

Power fell into the hands of a number of competing separate empires: police (Himmler), the second Four Year Plan (Göring), propaganda (Goebbels) and the Labour Front (Robert Ley). Inside their spheres, these Nazi leaders exercised considerable independence. Hitler, though ultimately supreme, was content to leave the detailed

**Figure 3** A cartoon by David Low entitled 'They salute with both hands now', which appeared in *Evening Standard*, 3 July 1934

work of administration to others. The system worked with ruthless efficiency.

A new spirit of hope, confidence, pride, determination and energy became apparent. Hitler offered:

- The **people** a new faith in the greatness and future of Germany. Order and discipline were re-established and the menace of Communism disappeared. People accepted Hitler and his strong government. Economic recovery was at the basis of Nazi success, for Hitler recognised that maximum support of the people was essential. This was achieved through a fall in unemployment, a rise in profits, control of inflation and a sound currency. Hitler's economic policies 1933–7 successfully achieved a fall in unemployment from the 6 million of January 1933 to 1 million in January 1935. It was a State-led revival based on construction of roads, land drainage and public works which aimed to give the people 'bread and work'. He introduced military conscription in 1935 and an official rearmament in the Four Year Plan of 1936. By 1939 there was a shortage of labour.

- **Industrialists**, freed of trade union restrictions, were given vast orders at profitable rates.
- **Junkers** were not totally won over, but they enjoyed advantages. Prices of products were fixed high above costs. They had State credit on easy terms and relieved of the fear of loss of their land.
- **Elites in the Army** were won over by Hitler's expansionist foreign policy. This provided opportunities for sons and reconciled the landowning nobility to the Nazis. Hitler showed supreme skill in handling the Army for the latter was the greatest factor in establishing his regime on a firm basis.

A reign of terror underpinned Hitler's rule. He used a combination of persuasion and deception in an organised form for the masses. This was combined with terror through the SA and SS, concentration camps, Gestapo, detention, imprisonment and execution. The SS became an instrument of tremendous power – respected and feared. It was a most active, relentless and merciless agent of coercion in police duties and the camps. The camps were the supreme agency of terror – Jews, communists and socialists were subjected to brutal discipline. The planned instruments of terror were used to crush opposition, deter criticism and discontent. People were successfully intimidated.

## Significant turning-point in the Third Reich's fortunes

The key date is 5 November 1937 – Hitler's meeting with his Chiefs of Staff and the German Foreign Minister in the Chancellery in Berlin. The conference was called to discuss the problem of steel shortage and its allocation between the armed services. Germany's resources of labour and raw materials were overstretched by 1937. The meeting turned into a discussion about expansion and war. Quite apart from any developing economic crisis Hitler was in any case determined, by 1937, to maintain or increase the revolutionary momentum of his movement in order to achieve his mission in world history. He exercised unrestricted control over the key areas of foreign policy following his success at dismantling the Versailles Settlement. He seems to have felt a need to move forward swiftly and radically. The conference is seen as a significant turning-point in the fortunes of the regime.

Hitler announced a new stage in foreign policy, namely the need to solve the 'problem of living space' by force by 1943 at the latest, with Austria and Czechoslovakia as targets in the near future. This would also broaden Germany's resource base, in preparation for a general war by about 1943. Representatives of the elites present at the Hossbach meeting made no objection to Hitler's aims concerning Austria and Czechoslovakia. The reservations of Blomberg, Neurath and Fritsch related only to timing, risks and the state of German rearmament.

The meeting was followed by a significant change in the balance of power. At the beginning of February 1938 the armed forces and the *Auswärtiges Amt* (Foreign Office) were reorganised after the dismissal of Blomberg, Neurath and Fritsch.

Hitler's control over foreign and defence policy and his own self-confidence were greatly strengthened by the sensational success of the *Anschluss* (union) of Austria with Germany which followed in March 1938. Economics Minister, Schacht, subsequently resigned leaving Göring in supreme command of the economy. Hitler completed the process of securing his power. More radical Nazis now came into control of power and the regime adopted a more aggressive policy at home and in foreign affairs.

## Germany at war, 1939–41

Most recent interpretations suggests that Hitler was not expecting to wage war until the mid-1940s. Even so Germany's commitment to a major war in the autumn of 1939 did not necessarily mean that militarily the country was doomed to fail.

Between September 1939 and November 1941 the German army won a number of victories which indicate the formidable military power Hitler had created. Within six weeks Hitler had made himself master of France and the Low Countries, repeating his earlier successes in Austria, Czechoslovakia and Poland. German territories were bordered by the three friendly countries of Spain, Italy and Russia (see Figure 1). Only Britain appeared to retain military and strategic independence.

Instead of defeating, or at least neutralising Britain, Hitler made the mistake of launching a war against Russia in July 1941 – 'Operation Barbarossa' – which had been planned in Directive Number 21 (18 December 1940). Vast tracts were occupied in the first months, but Hitler and his generals disagreed on tactics. This, with the Russian winter, contributed to Hitler's disastrous defeat in the winter of 1941. By the end of 1941 Hitler found himself fighting a war on two fronts.

December 1941 was also a turning-point in another sense. The Japanese attack on Pearl Harbor brought America into the war. Hitler allied with Japan against America. The war had become a world war. Hitler appeared to have lost his control of diplomatic and military events and to make decisions based on his own self-delusion rather than rational assessments of situations. The decisions made in December 1941 were a vital turning-point for German fortunes at war though this was not apparent at the time.

The winter of 1942–3 saw Germany defeated in Russia, at Stalingrad and in North Africa – defeats which could not be hidden from the people and which had a demoralising impact. From 1943 German strategy was defensive. Hitler was determined to protect Europe from invasion, but his military and political thinking became increasingly unrealistic.

- He believed that Germany continued to be superior so that defeat was impossible.
- He was concerned to create his new racial order and implement his views on race.

By 1943 the allied armies had joined forces in Africa and moved on to South Italy, while Russian troops had recovered the Ukraine. The fighting also started to have an impact on Germany – massive bombing raids created devastation and dislocation – so that it was clear by 1943 that Germany could not win the war. Allied demands for unconditional surrender prompted the 1944 July Plot by some generals of the *Wehrmacht* to assassinate Hitler. Its failure meant that the war was fought to the end. By May 1945 Germany was in ruins.

## Wilhelm FRICK *1877–1946*

He played an important role in helping Hitler in his early career because of his position as an official in the Munich Police Department. In 1930 Frick became the first Nazi to hold a ministerial position in a German state, as Minister of the Interior in Thuringia. Here he gave a foretaste of what Nazi rule would mean, by sacking officials with republican sympathies and appointing Nazis against established administrative procedures. During the Third Reich his influence gradually waned. He was executed after the Nuremberg War Crimes Trials.

## Ernst RÖHM *1887–1934*

A regular army officer who gave Hitler invaluable support in his early Munich days by acting as a link with the local army command. He became one of Hitler's closest associates, but was always independent. From 1925 he served as a military adviser in Bolivia, but was recalled by Hitler in 1930 to become Chief of Staff of the rapidly expanding SA. After the seizure of power he became a Reichminister and saw himself as a key figure in the Nazi revolution.

## Hermann GÖRING *1893–1946*

He joined the Nazi Party in 1923. In 1932 he was elected as Speaker of the Reichstag having convinced Hitler of his value as a 'high society Nazi'. He was popular but resented for his ambition and greed for power and wealth. He was concerned with his own pursuit of power rather than with any allegiance to Hitler or the Nazi Party. Göring's contributions to the State can be summed up in the various offices he amassed: he expanded his 'circle of duties' (1933–5) to include Reichstag President, Reich Minister of Aviation, Prussian Minister of the Interior, Head of the Gestapo, President of the

Prussian State Council, Commander-in-Chief of the Luftwaffe, and in 1936 Commissioner of the Four Year Plan. In 1937 he was denied the office of Minister in charge of the army, despite being a part of the intrigue to topple the previous holder. In 1939 he was appointed Hitler's successor, President of the Reich Defence Council and Reich Marshall. Between 1939 and 1942 he was dropped by Hitler so that by 1942 he was completely isolated. In 1943 he was arrested and sentenced to death at Nuremberg, but he committed suicide.

## Josef GOEBBELS *1898–1945*

One of the most astonishingly gifted propagandists of modern times, he was one of the few real powers complementing Hitler. It was Goebbels who developed the techniques of persuasion based on slogans, myths and images to 'package' Hitler. He was the originator of the term 'der Führer', and the creator and organiser of Hitler's cult. Hitler's position, both in the Nazi Party and as dictator, was enormously reinforced by Goebbels' propaganda. Hitler rewarded him, making him Gauleiter of Berlin, Minister of Information and Propaganda which gave him control of press, radio, cinema, theatre and literature. Goebbels showed himself to be a great master in the art of influencing the masses. He was probably the most loyal of all Nazi leaders to Hitler, Nazi ideology and Hitler's success. He was on very friendly terms with the Führer apart from brief interludes in 1937–8 and 1943–4. He and his family committed suicide with Hitler in the bunker in April 1945.

## Heinrich HIMMLER *1900–1945*

He joined the NSDAP in 1923. He stressed a code of honour and of family pedigree and marriage. He believed in a master race – an Aryan *Herrenvölk*. He became Reichsführer of the SS in 1935, the chief paramilitary elite group and Hitler's bodyguard. Under Himmler its membership grew from 500 to 50,000 and it created its own network of administration. In 1933 Himmler became President of Police in Munich and established a model camp at Dachau. Under Himmler a system of terror was carried out with great efficiency by his deputies. From its base in Bavaria the SS extended its control as the political police of Germany. Real power visibly shifted towards him and the SS, which determined the future face and history of the Third Reich. He had an evil reputation based on his association with the SS State, the extermination camps and system of terror.

### Rudolf HESS *1894–1987*

He had the title of deputy to the Führer from 1933 to 1941, but this did not bring him real power. He represented no danger to Hitler which was the reason for his selection as vice-Führer. Hess subordinated himself to Hitler and acted as his secretary (he wrote down *Mein Kampf).* His most important contribution to National Socialism was that he gave Hitler the concept of *lebensraum* (living space). He never craved power but existed solely to serve Hitler whom he regarded as saviour. Hess was sincere in his worship of Hitler. He was sentenced to life imprisonment at Nuremberg and died in mysterious circumstances as the last prisoner in Spandau prison in 1987.

### Martin BORMANN *1900–45?*

He was chief of staff to Hess until 1941 when he became the most powerful figure in Germany and in the Nazi Party. In 1930 he was put in charge of the Party's 'relief fund' which received funds from industrialists and bought up cheap land for Hitler. Nobody liked him, and everybody was afraid of him, but all needed him. In 1933 he became secretary at the ministry for Party affairs where his power was absolute – the minister, Hess, was only a figurehead. Mystery surrounds his fate after he disappeared during the final days of the war. Did he flee to South America or was he blown up by a road bomb during his escape?

## Reinhard HEYDRICH *1904–42*

Deputy chief of the Gestapo, he looked typically German, but was of Jewish blood. Heydrich aimed at nothing less than the leadership of the Third Reich. Heydrich was the originator of the plan to develop the police force of the Third Reich out of the SS, with him in control of the Party security police. In 1934 he became head of the political police, 1935 of the criminal police and by 1936, at the age of 32, was one of the most powerful men in Germany. In 1939, he organised the Reich Central Security Office nominally subordinate to Himmler, but it became independent and a part of his offices and activities. He developed a system of surveillance throughout Germany and Europe. He was given responsibility for destroying opposition from the churches and from the Jews. He devised the plan to make vast areas of the East available as an 'experimental field' for breeding. He devised the idea of forcing the Jewish communities to organise the Final Solution at its lowest levels. In 1941 Heydrich was sent to Prague, after Himmler and Bormann had joined forces to remove him from the centre of power and curtail his rapid rise which they regarded as threatening. Heydrich had some success with the workers and peasants in Prague but he was not popular. He died in 1942.

## Albert SPEER *1905–83*

He joined the Nazi Party in 1931 and in 1933 was appointed 'master builder' of the Third Reich, designing the monumental buildings of Nuremberg and Berlin. He refused to associate himself with the horrors of the regime and rejected an honorary rank in the SS. In 1941 he was appointed Minister of Armament and Munitions. He reshaped his ministry and under his direction armament production increased impressively even though he had to accept the necessity to employ slave labour from the camps. He was sentenced to 20 years' imprisonment at Nuremberg.

PART TWO

CHAPTER ONE

# DID HITLER HAVE THE SUPPORT OF MOST PEOPLE?

### Objectives

- **To understand the extent to which the Nazi Party represented in its structure the entire nation on a reduced scale**
- **To understand the extent to which Nazi success was due to widespread and genuine enthusiasm for their policies**
- **To evaluate and interpret primary source material by understanding and extracting information from it and reaching conclusions.**

## Hitler and the German people prior to 1933

### Who voted Nazi?

This is a difficult question. There is insufficient evidence relating to voting behaviour. Not surprisingly, after 1945 few people were prepared to admit that they had voted Nazi prior to 1933. Furthermore, there were no elections after March 1933. There are several ways in which the absence of such evidence can be partially overcome:

- performances of the main political parties – losses and gains
- local/regional breakdown of election results
- appeal of the Nazi programme
- the Party leader – his attitude and policy.

#### Performance of political parties

This involves a study of election results in order to plot trends. It should be noted that this line of enquiry is unreliable because both the electorate and voting behaviour change over time. This method becomes more reliable the closer together the elections occur, as in the case of Weimar elections in the period September 1930 to 5 March 1933 (see Figure 4 overleaf). Hitler and the Nazis did not aim to secure a majority in Reichstag elections. Such success was unlikely under a system of proportional representation which encouraged a multiplicity of small parties and interest groups. In this situation the success of the

NSDAP at the polls is impressive. Traditionally, 1930 is seen as the decisive date for the Nazi Party because of the opportunities offered by the onset of economic crisis and rising unemployment. More recently historians have pointed to the agricultural depression in 1928 as the significant turning-point when the Nazi Party emerged.

**DNVP (National(ist) Party)**
Formed in 1918 as a successor to the conservative parties of Imperial Germany. Its strength lay in North Germany and among Protestants and in the agricultural areas of East Prussia. It was monarchist, anti-republican and strongly nationalist. Between 1925 and 1928 the DNVP became reconciled to the republic to take part in government. This worked against it in the elections of 1928. After 1929 it adopted a more extreme anti-republican line cooperating with the Nazis. This could not halt the electoral decline of the party and the drift of its voters into the Nazi camp. Nevertheless, the party took part in the formation of the Hitler Cabinet, but this did not save it from the fate that befell all parties other than the NSDAP, namely dissolution in 1933.

**DVP (People's Party)**
Founded in 1918 as the more right wing of the two German Liberal parties, most German industrialists and business men supported this party. The DVP was losing electoral support even before 1928. After 1929 the party moved increasingly to the right, but this did not halt the drain of votes to the Nazis from 1930. By 1932 the DVP had been reduced to a small fringe party.

**DDP (Democratic Party)**
The more left wing of the two liberal parties was founded in 1918. Initially it made a strong showing, because many middle-class Germans believed it to be the only alternative to the socialist parties. But support for it was short-lived. By 1932 it polled only about 1 per cent of the vote in national elections.

**ZENTRUM (Centre Party)**
This was the party of German Catholics and survived as the most consistent of German parties until 1933. In the Weimar Republic

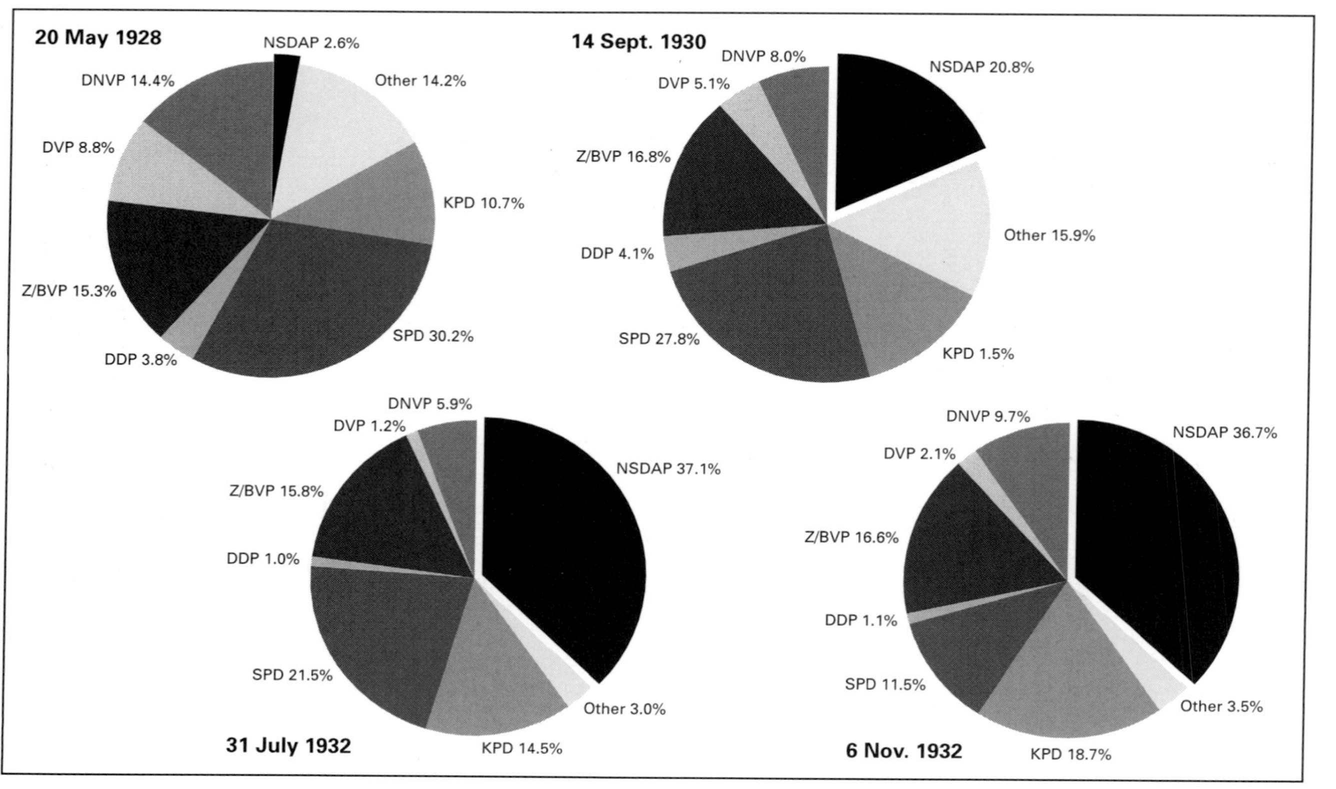


**Figure 4** Electoral breakthrough by the Nazi Party 1928–32

no government could be formed without it. It had both middle- and working-class support and its vote varied little throughout the Weimar period. It collaborated with the separate, more conservative Bavarian Catholic party, the BVP, in the Reichstag.

**SPD (Social Democratic Party)**
The SDP was the largest political party even in Imperial Germany. Its leaders shaped the course of events after the fall of the monarchy in 1918 and created the Weimar Republic. Although it was officially a Marxist party, it had always considered itself 'a party of revolution but not a party that makes revolution'. It was therefore essentially a reformist socialist party and from 1920 was competing with a strong and more radical Communist party on its left.

**KPD (Communist Party)**
Formed in 1918 by left-wing elements that had split off from the two main socialist parties, from 1920 its policy was increasingly determined from Moscow. It remained a small party throughout the 1920s gaining some support from defectors from the SPD. By 1932 unemployed German workers tended to vote KPD rather than SPD. There was a deep division in the German working class which contributed to the collapse of Weimar.

## Sources

**Table 2** Number of workers registered as unemployed

| Year | No. of unemployed |
|---|---|
| 1928 | 1,862,000 |
| 1929 | 2,850,000 |
| 1930 | 3,217,000 |
| 1931 | 4,886,000 |
| 1932 | 6,042,000 |

From J. Remak *The Nazi Years* (Prentice-Hall, 1969)

*...for five years I remained unemployed and I was broken both in body and spirit and I learned how stupid were all my dreams in those hard days at university. I was not wanted by Germany... then I was introduced to Hitler. You won't understand and I*

*cannot explain either because I don't know what happened, but life for me took on a tremendous new significance... I have committed myself, body, soul and spirit, to this movement... I can only tell you that I cannot go back. I cannot question, I am pledged. I beg you not to try to set up conflict in my mind.*

*Interview with unnamed member of the Nazi Party, 1936; quoted in J. Simkin* ***The Rise of Hitler*** *(Spartacus Education, 1986)*

The election results in Figure 4 show that, under the impact of depression and unemployment, the political parties right of centre were losing influence. Most of those who voted for the DNVP, DVP and DDP (see profiles) were drawn mainly from the Protestant middle class. Between 1928 and 1930 the Nazi Party concentrated on winning over their voters who were drawn from sections of the middle class. They met with success with these social groups; so the NSDAP came to have a high following among the middle and upper middle classes.

After 1930 they directed their attention to winning over the workers, who were disillusioned with democracy under the impact of high unemployment. They set up a National Socialist Factory Cell Organisation (the NSBO), but it had limited success. The Nazis failed substantially in their efforts to court the industrial working class traditionally mobilised by the left-wing parties and the trade union movement. Nevertheless, most commentators calculate that somewhere around 30 per cent of the Nazi voters were blue-collar workers; some put it higher. The NSDAP made many converts among the craft sections of the working class employed in smaller firms and in less heavily industrialised smaller towns or rural areas. They had not previously been effectively organised either by the parties of the Left or by trade unions. It is important to realise that it was the complexity of the German working class which explains the presence of a working-class Nazi vote.

There is evidence that the decline of the SPD was not only to the benefit of the KPD, but also of the NSDAP. This still means that workers were under-represented in the Nazi movement in relation to their proportion in the population as a whole, around 46 per cent. It does, however, give support to Hitler's claim to be the leader of a mass movement whose broad-based support had risen above class barriers. The outcome of these political regroupings was that by 1932 the parties associated with the Weimar Republic found that their vote had been taken over by the Nazi Party. By July 1932 only the DNVP among the parties mentioned retained any sizeable numbers of voters. Politics was becoming increasingly polarised though there was continuing support for the Catholic Centre. It was the rise in the KPD vote which contributed to Hitler being offered the chancellorship in 1933. His conservative, nationalist supporters expected him, as leader of the largest party in the Reichstag, to stave off a potential challenge from the KPD.

**Local/regional breakdown of results**

Study of the percentage of votes cast in the different electoral districts of Germany shows the significance of religion and industrialisation in determining support.

The Nazis could mobilise the population in the Protestant and predominantly rural areas of the North German plain. They were weakest in the big cities and in the industrial areas generally, particularly in the predominantly Catholic ones. The voters most resistant to the Nazis were those who normally supported the Catholic Centre Party or its Bavarian counterpart, the BVP. While Catholics formed about 35 per cent of the German population, support for the two Catholic parties had settled down to around 15 per cent in the Weimar years. It did not drop below this level in the elections of the early 1930s, except for the last one in March 1933, when Hitler was already Chancellor. Centre Party and BVP voters were usually practising, churchgoing Roman Catholics. The clergy preached from the pulpit that support for National Socialism was sinful, because of its racial doctrines. In the final months before Hitler's arrival in power, the leaders of the Centre Party unsuccessfully negotiated with him about the formation of a coalition and this began to confuse Catholic voters. Nevertheless, the Nazi electoral performance in Catholic areas like the Rhineland and Lower and Upper Bavaria remained below the national average.

The Nazis were strong in those border areas like East Prussia where their nationalism appealed to a population resentful of loss of territory through the Versailles Treaty. These areas were also, except in Upper Silesia, predominantly Protestant. Nazi gains were limited in the

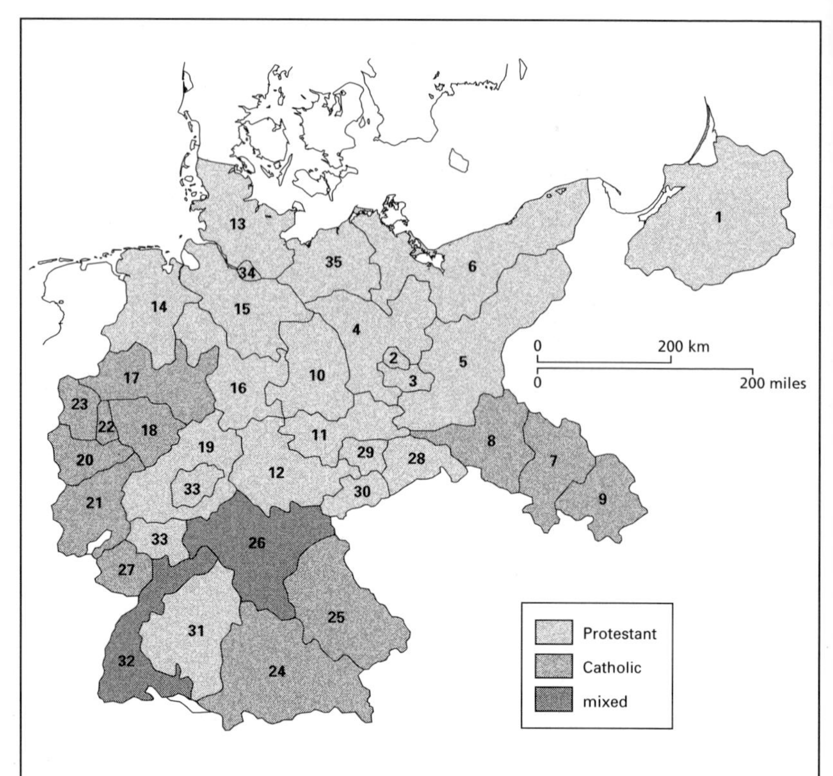


**Protestant**

- **1** East Prussia
- **2** Berlin
- **3** Potsdam II
- **4** Potsdam I
- **5** Frankfurt an der Oder
- **6** Pomerania
- **10** Magdeburg
- **11** Merseburg
- **12** Thuringia
- **13** Schleswig-Holstein
- **14** Weser-Ems
- **15** East Hanover
- **16** South Hanover-Brunswick
- **19** Hesse-Nassau
- **28** Dresden-Bautzen
- **29** Leipzig
- **30** Chemnitz-Zwickau
- **31** Wurttemberg
- **33** Hesse-Darmstadt
- **34** Hamburg
- **35** Mecklenburg

**Catholic**

- **7** Breslau
- **8** Liegnitz
- **9** Oppeln
- **17** Westphalia-North
- **18** Westphalia-South
- **20** Cologne-Aachen
- **21** Koblenz-Tier
- **22** Dusseldorf East
- **23** Dusseldorf West
- **24** Upper Bavaria-Swabia
- **25** Lower Bavaria
- **27** Palatinate

**Mixed**

- **26** Franconia
- **32** Baden

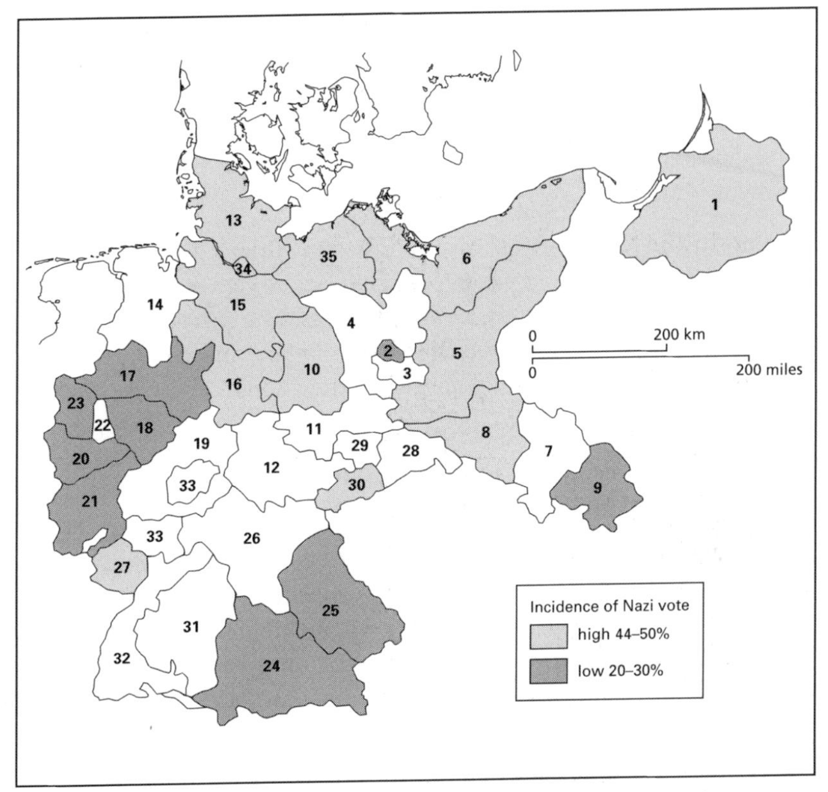


**Figure 5** Comparison of strength of the Nazi Party vote (July 1932) according to Germany's religious divide (Source: J. Noakes and G. Pridham (eds) *A Documentary Reader: Nazism 1919–45* vol. 1)

cities where the SPD and the KPD held on to most of their support from the factory-based working class. If such cities were strongly Catholic – such as Cologne – there was a double reason restricting Nazi gains. Cologne was, in fact, one of the electoral districts where the Nazi vote always remained among the lowest.

## Appeal of the Nazi programme

This was directed at those voters whom Hitler believed to be the core of the Nazi vote. The main limitation to this line of enquiry is that there was no consumer research carried out at the time and no one in retrospect was prepared to admit having voted for the NSDAP.

Hitler had great skill in manipulating an audience. He was one of the greatest speakers of the twentieth century. He had supreme control over audiences, appealing to their emotions with his speeches on purity of blood and racial inferiority. A study of Nazi election propaganda posters suggest that the appeal of the NSDAP rested on the following factors:

- **Cult of the leader** – this was promoted in Hitler's dress, the content of speech and visual presentation, along with messages associated with 'Germany awake'. Leaders were surrounded by SA bodyguards, who presented the image of a disciplined military formation. These devices appealed to the young.
- **Nationalism** was stirred by the 'stab-in-the-back' tradition and an anti-Communist platform which attracted the support of the nationalist, patriotic elements.
- **Appeal to the youth of Germany** was based on the promise of action, comradeship and a sense of idealism and commitment to a cause. Young people believed they were taking part in the rebirth of Germany in a more direct way than those who belonged to other parties. Propaganda messages were simple, depending on action rather than thought. A recurring message was to 'suffer pain'.
- The **concept of struggle** – many Germans shared Hitler's personal philosophy of 'struggle' and the will of the individual (see Figure 6). A culture of violence spread fostered by fears of a 'red' revolution from the SPD or KPD.
- **Anti-semitism** – Jews were presented as an inferior race and the source of all evil in society. Hitler claimed that the Jews undermined the nation. In reality, Jews accounted for a small percentage of Germany's population. They were prominent in cultural life and the professions. As a result of their prominence as traders and shopkeepers, they were perceived to be wealthy.

**Party leader: his attitude and policy**

This line of enquiry is concerned with the style and image used by the Nazis to fight election campaigns. Before coming to power the Nazis used a number of positive messages in their posters and speeches. They aimed at a breadth of appeal across social groups, but especially to the

**Figure 6** Nazi propaganda poster: *National Sozialismus* ('National Socialism: The Organised Will of the Nation'), 1932

unemployed and ex-soldiers. 'Bread and Work' was a recurring theme appealing to the millions of unemployed (see Figure 7, on page 36). Hitler was portrayed as 'our last hope' and the saviour of the family.

Another theme was 'Germany on the move' which embraced the concept of struggle, 'we are building' but 'we have to fight to do it' (note the bandage on the soldier's head in Figure 6). The image was presented of Hitler as leader of Germany. One strong message of 1931–2 was the drive to get rid of big business, Communists and Socialists – 'we are mucking out the stables' (see Figure 8, on page 36).

Nazi propaganda was successful in cultivating an image of a party which was youthful and radical, nationalist and both anti-semitic and anti-Marxist. It appeared to be sympathetic to small businesses and peasants, but not hostile to the landowners. However, it is misleading to say that Hitler and his party conquered the masses. There is the danger of concentrating on the techniques of persuasion and not looking at the programme. To vote for the Nazi manifesto was not an irrational act, as has been suggested. Many groups voted out of self-interest rather than being persuaded by propaganda. Other groups remained resistant. Propaganda was not the determining factor but the

**Figure 7** Nazi propaganda poster: *Arbeit und Brot* ('Work and Bread'), November 1932

**Figure 8** Nazi propaganda poster: *Wir Bauern Miften Aus* ('We Farmers are cleaning out the dung') (1932)

failure of the Weimar system. It was important in mobilising support in opposition, but it could not alone have sustained the Nazi Party. Nazi policies reflected many aspirations of large sections of populations; propaganda reinforced existing attitudes and beliefs. The success of these tactics of aiming to draw support from right across the social spectrum can be shown from an analysis of those who supported Nazism. (Compare the chart on Nazi support in Part One and Figure 9.)

## Who were the Nazis?

Electoral support for the Nazis is not the same as membership of the party. Voting does not require effort and is secret. Being a Party member meant putting on a uniform and being an activist, possibly at some personal danger. Historians have more reliable evidence on membership because of the availability of party membership records.

Various efforts have been made to identify the typical Nazi. A comprehensive survey of members and leaders of the Nazi Party for the period 1919–46 was carried out by Michael Kater (see Figure 10). He concludes that membership was male dominated and lower middle class

| Social basis of Nazism | Motive |
|---|---|
| Ex-soldiers | Resented the humiliation of defeat during the First World War. Many joined ex-soldiers groups of *Freikorps* who found it difficult to settle as civilians and find work. |
| Middle class | Resented the loss of income, savings and security as a result of the collapse of the economy 1928–33. Attracted by anti-communist propaganda. |
| Upper middle class/the elites | Were disillusioned with the Weimar Republic and did not want a return to parliamentary government. As early as 1927 some elements among the elites had supported National Socialism. This was true of the large landowners whose organisation, the *Reichslandbund*, had been infiltrated by the Nazis. |
| 'Big business' | Sections of industry were attracted to the Nazi programme of economic self-sufficiency and saw advantage in a big rearmament programme. They feared the advance of Communism and were disillusioned with the Weimar Republic and did not want a return to parliamentary democracy. However, they were not 'the authors of Hitler's chancellorship'. They did not support Hitler or the NSDAP in large numbers for the activities of the left wing of the party alienated them. |
| Peasantry/ small farmers | They thought that the Nazis would restore the prosperity of the farming community and were attracted by the promise of land reforms. |
| Working class e.g. village craft workers | Attracted by Hitler's promise of bread and work and the socialist content of National Socialism which implied reforms for their benefit. |
| All classes | Individuals voted because they were nationalist minded; were hostile to the Jews. Some of the criminal classes and other social misfits sought an outlet for their criminal instincts. Opportunists looked for a means to improve their own status. |

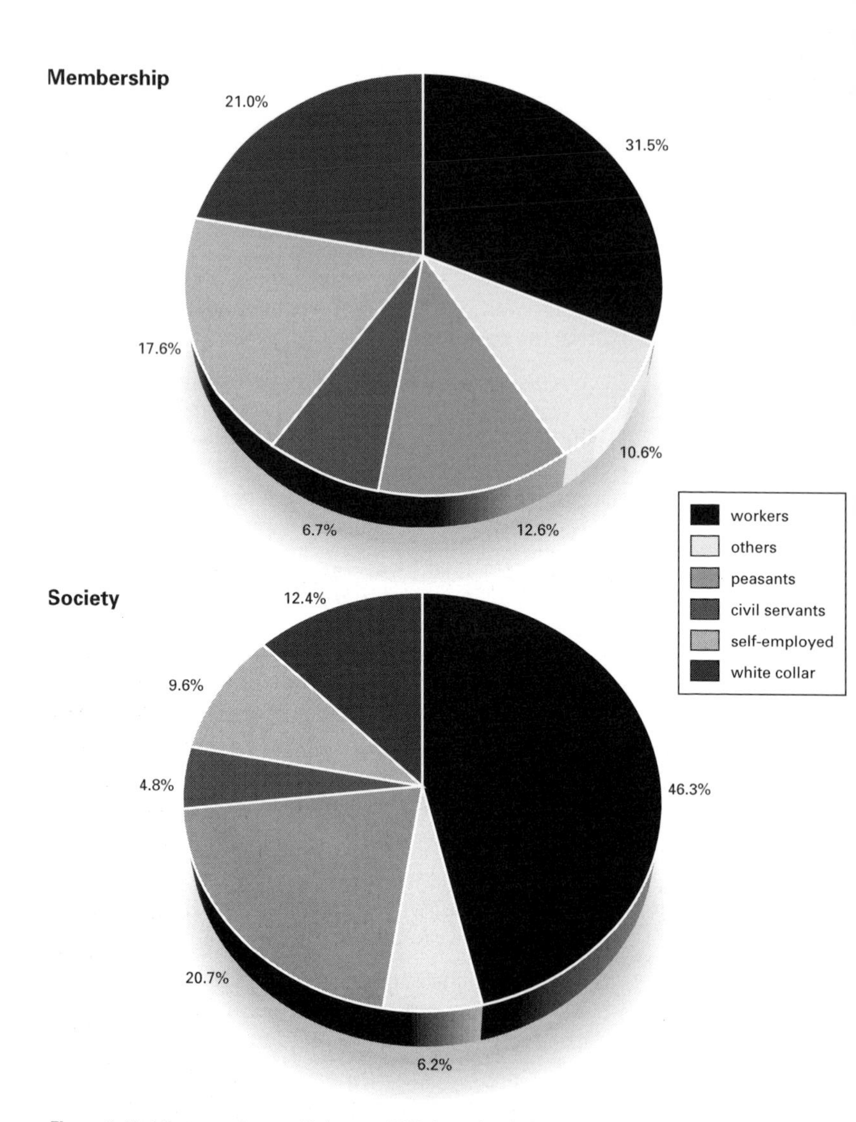


**Figure 9** Nazi Party members on 31 January 1933 shown in relation to their percentage in society

with the working class under-represented and the elite groups over-represented. Kater argues that there were no major social differences between party officials and the rank and file. Differences developed after 1933 when more women became members and social divisions grew with the over-representation of elite groups.

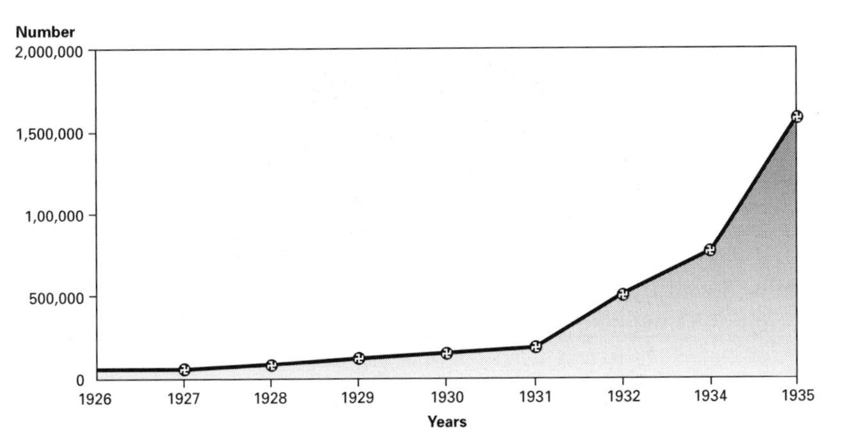


**Figure 10** Growth in Nazi Party membership between the years 1927 and 1935

# Hitler and the German people after 1933

After 1933 the image of German society conveyed by Nazi propaganda in newsreels and the press was of mass enthusiasm and commitment. However, in trying to understand how the people really felt during these years the historian is faced with serious problems for an independent public opinion did not exist. Freedom of speech and assembly were suppressed and there were no opinion polls. Terror was always in the background and was ruthlessly applied when necessary. Elections and ***plebiscites*** were rigged and the media was strictly controlled. Newspapers are of limited value as a source because they were censored and controlled by Goebbels' Propaganda Ministry.

### Key Term

A **plebiscite** a direct vote of all electors on a particular issue, such as to which state an area should belong or a change in the constitution.

This situation also posed problems for the regime itself which was anxious to know what the German people were thinking and feeling. A number of agencies were responsible for finding out popular opinion. The Security Service of the SS (SD), the Gestapo, the Party, regional government offices and the judicial authorities all prepared reports on public morale and the popular response to such issues as food shortages and the employment situation. Such reports were concerned about active resistance and/or opposition and were based on information from informers scattered throughout the population. Despite obvious problems of interpretation, the reports of these agencies provide an important source.

Another important source on popular opinion is the reports of the exiled Social Democratic Party's contact men in Germany. These were former SPD members who supplied regular information of life in the Third Reich. This was used for the monthly reports prepared by the SOPADE, the exiled SPD in Switzerland. Again, they provide a remarkable source for attitudes to the regime among various sections of the population. Although the regime had institutionalised terror, it is clear that it operated on a remarkable degree of consent from the people. A number of factors account for this.

### Führer myth

Central to this was the image of Hitler as the Führer who was above party and politics, a leader who dedicated himself to the service of the people and provided them with the leadership they had sought since 1918. However, this desire for positive leadership had to be accompanied by successes.

### Success of the regime's policies

Everybody benefited, to some extent, from Nazi policies. The fall in unemployment won over the workers, while the restoration of Germany's position as a European power attracted others (see page 41). A crucial element in popular consent to the regime was the fact that Nazism embodied, in an extreme form, many of the basic attitudes of a large section of the German people. It was not just nationalism and militarism which appealed to the people, many shared the essential conservatism of the regime. There was wide support for the regime's hostility towards unpopular minorities, and for its firm line against tramps, homosexuals, antisocials, criminals and the workshy.

### Control of people's lives

The regime understood the importance of organising the people and of controlling not only their work lives through the German Labour Front, but also leisure. Clubs and private associations which had been characteristic of German life were put under the control of reliable Party members as part of the policy of national coordination (*Gleichschaltung*). The effect of this Nazi technique of organisation was that people withdrew from political involvement. They were not encouraged to ask questions and many did not question the regime until the 1939–45 war.

## Who opposed the Nazis?

Formal and organised political resistance against the regime was limited after 1933 because of the quick disappearance of a multi-party democracy. Political opposition became concentrated in small groups and individuals. Historians writing in the years soon after 1945 tended to take a biased and hostile view of those who opposed the regime. The plot by the generals in July 1944 to blow up Hitler and his chiefs of staff at a crucial war planning meeting was described by the *New York Times* as not what one would normally expect within an officers' corps and a civilised state. The use of a bomb was described as 'the typical weapon of the underworld'. This attitude stemmed from the belief that the generals, faced with defeat, were acting only from self-interest and were looking to protect themselves against recriminations by the allies for their failure to oppose the Nazi regime. Given this view, it was believed that no opposition to Hitler worth speaking of ever existed. The Germans were seen as having voluntarily associated themselves with the rule of Nazi criminals.

In many respects this was a distorted and misrepresented view. It is true that many Germans, enthusiastically or obediently, supported Hitler and his government despite the regime's evil character. The reasons for this are varied; many were aware of an apparent improvement in their economic and social conditions with the fall in unemployment and public welfare schemes. The regime also played on people's emotions with its propaganda messages of belonging to the people's community. They responded positively to Hitler's success in foreign policy which led to a recovery of all that had been surrendered at Versailles: rearmament and reoccupation of the Rhineland, along with acquisition of Austria and of Czechoslovakia. Hitler further benefited from the apparent willingness of European statesmen to recognise these acquisitions and negotiate with the regime. Equally, thousands 'submitted' for reasons other than that they felt attracted by the system or expected to gain from it. They had become disenchanted with the political process associated with democracy and preferred to retreat inwards to family and home. Others were intimidated by the presence of terror aroused by the secret police or because they were defenceless, and without legal remedy. The regime also acted promptly taking those who would have offered the most energetic resistance into 'protective custody' or forcing opponents to flee Germany.

Despite this, there were those who were prepared to oppose, though such opposition was tempered by the need for secrecy to protect family and friends. Allied contact with underground movements in Germany indicated that opposition to the regime extended from Right to extreme Left in terms of its political composition.

**Scope of Nazi opposition**

- **The Left** (*e.g.* Social Democrats, Communists and trade unionists) – the bulk of German socialists were opposed on ideological grounds, reinforced by persecution. Activity consisted of informal contacts in houses, smuggling books to each other rather than political activity which could be easily penetrated by the Gestapo. Workers were encouraged to commit acts of sabotage in factories. The Left carried out an anti-Nazi pamphlet and poster campaign.

- **Individual priests** of the Catholic (800) and Lutheran Churches (300–400) – they opposed the regime's anti-Christian and racial policies though there was no unity among Protestants. Throughout the 1930s Catholics organised local grassroots campaigns against Nazi attempts to ban the display of crucifixes in Catholic schools and to replace them with portraits of the Führer. The resistance among the Churches deterred the regime from extreme measures such as withdrawal of the edict to ban the display of the crucifix in schools in Munster in 1936. Such Catholic opposition was the only one to achieve visible success. Government response to opposition from the clergy after 1939 was to call them up for war service. However, opposition from within the Churches gave them a new inner vitality and provoked a Christian solidarity which was a distinctive feature of German opposition and allowed the Church to recover lost ground. People saw attendance at Church services as an expression of opposition.

- **Traditional Conservative groups** (*e.g.* professional people, members of the Civil Service) – the Right acted through moral conviction, and a revulsion against Nazi activities which were viewed as both anti-German and anti-human. The 'White Rose' letters were issued as part of the pamphlet campaign against the regime. A quarter of the student body did not join the National Socialist Students' League and there was a student revolt in Munich in 1943. They were joined by some intellectuals and university teachers. A resistance cell known as 'Red Chapel' was uncovered in Göring's Air Ministry in August 1942, while within the Intelligence and Counter-Espionage Department, the Combined Staff placed a protective veil over leading members of the department who were opponents of the regime.

- The **Army** represented the only significant opposition before 1939. A number of plots were planned to get rid of Hitler – such as in 1938 during the Czechoslovakian crisis, but were abandoned in the face of his success at Munich. In 1938 Hitler purged the High Command of those who questioned his strategy and tactics and assumed personal control over the Army. However, the generals' opposition stemmed more from their dislike of war, particularly against Russia, than hostility to the regime. It was the prospect of defeat at the hands of the Allies which finally led to the plot by some high-ranking army officers to blow up Hitler in July 1944.

- **Young people** formed groups such as Edelweiss and the Packs; 2,000 were organised in the Packs by 1939.

- **Individuals** – pogroms against the Jews brought people of humanitarian outlook together in opposition. Resistance groups were found in Munich, Augsberg and Berlin. In the latter city they were known as 'Uncle Emil' and were responsible for giving food and successfully hiding 5,000 Jews, obtaining forged papers and secret transport for persons wanted by the Gestapo. According to the Americans, from 1945 onwards when they examined one million applicants for employment in the US zone, 50 per cent showed no evidence of Nazi activity. Even though this is an over-estimate, the percentage of non-Nazis remained surprisingly high.

## Difficulties faced by the Opposition/Resistance

Germany lacked strong revolutionary traditions and there was the problem of finding effective means to oppose the regime. Nazi control worked very well, though it took time to develop the instruments to institutionalise terror. After 1935 the Gestapo improved its techniques and infiltrated Leftist ranks. Research shows that the secret police depended on informers and the cooperation of the people. The Gestapo exploited the pro-Hitler sympathies. Charges of acting treasonably proved to be a powerful control on the actions of soldiers and aristocrats who feared the label of 'traitor', especially after 1939. Socialists feared that their opposition would lead the regime to react by destroying Socialism among the working class, and they wanted to avoid blame of being responsible for its final destruction. Lack of unity among social groups, combined with lack of experience in forms of political agitation, further discouraged cooperation. The emigration of many of those who would have opposed the regime removed, at a crucial time, those who could have moulded opinion and events. The 1939–45 war made the situation worse for the emergency and bitter conflict in the East legitimised the State's use of terror.

## Types of opposition/resistance

Faced by these various difficulties German opposition took shape in various forms long before the war and reached its climax in an attempt to prevent war. By 1937 opposition was a civil resistance because it was recognised that under the Nazi regime unarmed resistance had little hope of success. It was recognised that success depended on breaking the chains of the SS and Gestapo. Some men joined the Party and took office to build opposition from inside the regime. Such people in 'high places' preserved their inner independence and later participated in active opposition. The Secretary of State in the Prussian Ministry of the Interior, Bismarck, protested and then resigned over the illegality of persecution. Anti-Nazis could often be found in 'high places' where they worked effectively under the cloak of their membership of the ruling classes and even under the protection of a high position in the Gestapo or SS, or among Ribbentrop's closest entourage at the Foreign Ministry. The Civil Service contained many opponents, such as Gördeler, who used their position to organise escape routes. Where they existed within the police they arranged escapes for intended victims of the Gestapo by entering such names in the missing persons' files. Others could be found working in small groups within the Ministries of the Interior, Justice, Labour and in local government where they used their position to sabotage Nazi law enforcement.

Many fell back on informal acts of defiance over some specific disagreement. Letters of protest were written, and policies were obstructed at great danger. Any form of dissent was seen as a political crime, punished by imprisonment, fines and 're-education'. In some cases these individual acts of resistance flared up into more organised resistance, as in the successful protest over the banning of the crucifix and of the euthanasia programme. There were numerous acts of petty dissent which were non-political and particularly effective among workers. The latter sought to improve their bargaining position and defend their living standards and skills. Workers embarked on acts of passive resistance, such as working to rule, sabotage and absenteeism through sickness. In Germany's bureaucratic system such acts of dissent were effective and friction arose between Nazi officials and those who implemented instructions. Business people also resisted, and in the state-led economy of the late 1930s isolated industrialists, managers and engineers were removed or went into voluntary exile in Switzerland.

## Reaction of the regime

The regime reacted promptly with public acts of punishment. It is difficult to estimate the size of the opposition, but some historians have suggested that of the 1,200,000 Germans interned in the camps, 500,000 to 600,000 were political prisoners. It is interesting to note that between 1943 and 1945 it took 40,000 of the Gestapo to 'neutralise' opponents. The death sentence was imposed for political reasons, in possibly 12,000 cases. Though the reliability of these figures is questionable, they nevertheless give some indication of the scope of passive and active resistance to the regime.

## TASKS

*What makes good notes?*

- Think out your own structure to give good basic knowledge.
- Devise a system of abbreviations.
- Omit unnecessary words.
- Leave out details which add nothing to the understanding of the main points identified in the activity guide.
- Use side headings to help comprehension, the learning of information and the ability to use it.

Now make your own notes using the following as a guide.

**1 Who voted Nazi?**

Read the relevant sections and refer to the statistical and visual evidence.

**a** Identify the political parties mentioned in Figure 4.

**b** Over the period as a whole which parties at each of the elections 1928–33:

i lost seats

ii gained seats

iii remained stable?

**c** Which parties lost votes to the Nazis? Why may this have taken place?

**d** Did the Nazi Party represent in its structure the entire nation on a reduced scale? Explain your answer.

**2 Did the NSDAP vote vary between regions?**

Study the regional breakdown of the Nazi vote at its peak in a 'free' election – July 1932 – against the background of the religious affiliation and industrial/rural breakdown of the German states.

**a** Which regions showed:

i a high percentage of votes cast for the Nazis

ii the lowest support?

Record your findings in a table format.

**b** What possible explanations can you suggest to explain these trends?

**3 What role was played by the Nazi programme and party leader?**

Study the election propaganda posters and the table of Nazi supporters (pages 35–6).

**a** On the basis of these posters whom did Hitler believe to be the core of the NSDAP vote?

**b** What did the appeal of the Nazi Party rest upon?

## TASKS

**c** What positive propaganda messages did the Nazis employ before coming to power?

You might find it useful to draw up profiles of the people who represented the core of the Nazi vote. Include an analysis of the reasons why different groups of people voted NSDAP.

**4 Who joined the NSDAP as members?**

How valid is it to claim that '*support for the Nazis came disproportionately from the middle classes and elite who felt threatened by the crisis in the years 1929–33*'?

**5 Hitler and the German people after 1933**

**a** Why did masses of Germans enthusiastically or obediently support Hitler and his government despite the regime's undoubted criminal character?

**b** Who were the opponents of the regime? Why?

**c** What forms did resistance take and with what effect?

**d** What difficulties were faced by those who opposed the regime in organised formal acts?

# HITLER – A WEAK DICTATOR OR MASTER OF THE THIRD REICH?

## Objectives

- To understand the relationship between Hitler and other leading Nazis
- To understand that historians can hold different opinions about the past which can lead to differing interpretations of the role of Hitler.

## The nature of the Nazi regime/Hitler's leadership

You might already have some impression of Hitler even if you have not studied the Nazi period. He is often presented as an absurd little man. Certainly cartoonists of the day ridiculed him in this manner (see Figure 3 on page 18). Such a view disguises the complex personality of the man who had the power to dominate and rouse an audience and the basis of his fatal attraction. Many accepted his 'dictatorship' and remained loyal to the end. As you will have learned from Part One, Germany appeared to be a one-party state under the sole rule of Hitler. Hitler established an extraordinarily powerful dictatorship which had considerable popular support especially in the 1930s. It was underpinned by an effective police apparatus whilst his rivals were ineffective. Goebbels' propaganda aimed at creating a Hitler myth, which emphasised his far-seeing political genius. This myth generated great support and helped him to inspire his followers with devotion and enthusiasm. Hitler's all-powerful position as Führer was made explicit on a number of occasions.

### Source

1 *At the head of the Reich stands the leader of the NSDAP as leader of the German Reich for life.*

2 *He is, on the strength of being the leader of the NSDAP, leader and Chancellor of the Reich. As such he embodies simultaneously, as Head of State, supreme State power, and, as chief of the government, the central functions of the whole Reich*

*administration. He is Head of State, and chief of the Government in one person. He is Commander in Chief of all the armed forces of the Reich.*

*3 The Führer and Reich Chancellor is the... delegate of the German people, who... decides the outward form of the Reich, its structure and general policy.*

*4 The Führer is supreme judge of the nation... There is no position in the area of constitutional law in the Third Reich independent of the ... will of the Führer.*

*1938 speech by Hans Frank, head of the Nazi Association of Lawyers and of the Academy of German law, quoted in J. Noakes and G. Pridham (eds),* ***Nazism 1919–1945, A Documentary Reader****, vol. II (1984)*

Historians writing after the Second World War focused on Hitler and the nature of his dictatorship. Hitler was portrayed as a leader who dictated events and who established an ascendancy over all who came into contact with him, even though they might disagree with his decisions. He was seen as master in the Third Reich.

Gradually, historical research showed this idea to need revision. Far from seeing him as master, historians wrote of a man remote from public affairs. Hitler was 'unwilling to take decisions, frequently uncertain, exclusively concerned with upholding his prestige and personal authority, influenced in the strongest fashion by his current entourage, in some respects a weak dictator' wrote Hans Mommsen in 1971.

The debate centres on the philosophical argument of the role of the individual in shaping the course of history. Commentators on the Third Reich have tended to get divided into two 'schools' of thought:

- **Intentionalists** stress that the essential political decisions were taken by Hitler. He was the prime mover in domestic and foreign policy. So important was the leadership principle that they have equated Nazism with Hitlerism.

- **Structuralists** stress the limitations on Hitler's freedom of action as a result of forces operating within the State. They argue that, under Hitler, Nazi Germany suffered from a leadership crisis. From the mid 1930s Hitler abandoned the normal business of government. He resorted to extreme working methods and lifestyles, a development which was commented upon by contemporaries.

## Sources

*When, I would often ask myself, did he really work? Little was left of the day; he rose late in the morning, conducted one or two official conferences; but from the subsequent dinner on he more or less wasted his time until the early hours of the evening. His rare appointments in the late afternoon were imperilled by his passion for looking at building plans. The adjutants often asked me: 'please don't show any plans today'... In the eyes of the people Hitler was the Leader who watched over the nation day and night. This was hardly so... According to my observations, he often allowed a problem to mature during the weeks when he seemed to be entirely taken up with trivial matters. Then after the 'sudden insight' came, he would spend a few days of intensive work giving final shape to his solution... Once he had come to a decision, he lapsed again into his idleness.*

*Albert Speer's account of Hitler's inefficient lifestyle; quoted in D. G. Williamson* ***The Third Reich*** *(AWL, 1982)*

*Ministerial skill in the Third Reich consisted in making the most of a favourable hour or minute when Hitler made a decision, this often taking the form of a remark thrown out casually, which then went its way as an 'Order of the Führer'.*

*State Secretary in the Foreign Office, Ernst von Weizsäcker* ***Memoirs*** *(1951); quoted in A. Bullock* ***Hitler, A Study in Tyranny*** *(Penguin, 1961)*

Hitler did not actively intervene in government, and his withdrawal made the machinery of government more chaotic because important decisions were not taken. Government disintegrated into a number of competing personal empires such as those controlled by Göring, Himmler and Goebbels. Hitler became more dispensable in this very personal system. He rarely issued written orders and the absence of such evidence has further contributed to the debate on Hitler's role in decision-making. (We will return to this when we look at the regime's policies against the Jews.) In this situation there appeared to be administrative inefficiency combined with improvised decision-making. Real power seemed to rest with individuals concerned with a personal pursuit of power.

Historians' views on the role of Hitler can be summarised as follows:

| Intentionalists | Structuralists |
|---|---|
| Some intentionalist historians: Hugh Trevor-Roper, *The Last Days of Hitler* (1946) Alan Bullock, *Hitler, A Study in Tyranny* (1952) | Some structuralist historians: Hans Mommsen, *Civil Servants in the Third Reich* (1961) Martin Broszat, *The Hitler State* (1969) |
| Saw Hitler as Master. They stress the centrality of Hitler's personality, ideas and strengths. They claim that National Socialism can be called Hitlerism. | Saw Hitler as 'weak', failing to give clear planning and consistent direction. This led to the collapse of ordered government and self-destruction. |
| Regard Hitler as having predetermined goals especially in foreign policy. | Emphasise 'institutional anarchy' and leadership chaos. Power was distributed among many. Hitler's own authority was only one important element. |
| Saw hostility between rival groups as being resolved solely in the key position of the Führer. | Saw chaotic government structure as a consequence of Hitler's skilful 'divide and rule' strategy. |
| Saw Hitler as central to foreign and race policy. | Saw Hitler as sanctioning pressures operating from different forces within the regime rather than creating policy.<br><br>Still give Hitler a central role. His anti-semitism, anti-Bolshevism and *lebensraum* acted as ideals/symbols.<br><br>Mommsen wrote that Hitler was a propagandist, aware of presenting an image and exploiting the opportune moment. Statements about ideology were seen as propaganda rather than firm statements of intent. |

### How do we reconcile these different interpretations?

Historians now recognise the limits of Hitler's powers, for he did not enjoy absolute authority. The administrative structure of the Third Reich was complex. Hitler ruled through his trusted henchmen, but could not ignore his dependence on the traditional elites. He was not prepared to carry out a radical purge of the civil service because he was unwilling to jeopardise his relationship with the elites on which the regime was based. He was also unwilling to risk disrupting the major priorities of a return to full employment and the introduction of a major rearmament programme, particularly as the elites were prepared to cooperate with the new order. They considered that the regime's goals coincided with their own. The elites controlled the army, civil service, industry and finance. They continued to run the existing government departments and a parallel system of Nazi-controlled ministries was developed alongside. The cabinet did not operate, so the Reich Chancellery coordinated activities. Hitler only took decisions when absolutely necessary. The term '**polycratic**' has been applied to this system of government. It describes a complex power structure in which Hitler's personal authority was only one element.

However, Hitler expected total loyalty and all power rested with him. All nominees for posts at all levels (even village) had to be referred to him for selection and appointment. He regarded his appointments as his agents, dealing with them directly; while they in turn regarded Hitler as their immediate superior. There are no examples of major policy decisions by Hitler being successfully opposed by subordinates or by the Party. He was determined not to be restricted in any way or to have a rival. It would be misleading to view Hitler as a weak dictator.

## Relationship between Hitler and other leading Nazis

Hitler had a personal entourage, many members being drawn from the earliest days of the movement. He surrounded himself with a mixed crew chosen for their ability rather than for their personal friendship with him. At its most extensive in the heyday of the Third Reich 1933 to 1941 it numbered around 60–70, composed of ***Gauleiters,***

***Reichsleiters*** and prominent SA and SS officials. This group can be narrowed down to a much smaller one of about 12 having easy access to Hitler at all times. These were all long-serving Party members, the same age as Hitler and mostly with administrative experience in the Party. The composition of this 'kitchen cabinet' changed over the years, but included Göring, Himmler, Goebbels, Hess and Bormann (see picture gallery in Part One). Hitler's promotion of individuals on the basis of intuitive judgement rather than on hard fact increased still further the degree of dependence of those fortunate to win his favour.

## Key Terms

***Gauleiter*** – a regional Nazi Party leader responsible for all political and economic activities, civil defence and the mobilisation of labour in his district.

***Reichsleiter*** – a high-ranking member of the Nazi Party.

Hitler used a system of rewards and punishments to bind his key members to his rule. He was the tactician who organised the Party, created its ideology and masterminded its campaign for power. He was the dominant focal point and others accepted his dictatorship. He possessed superior talents confirmed by the struggle for power in the Party and his power of suggestion over men and the masses. Hitler welded the diffuse elements together so that everything came exclusively from the Führer himself. He demanded, and achieved until shortly before his death, absolute obedience. He also ensured his supremacy and unchallenged leadership by fostering an anarchy of rivalries in the struggle for power among leading Nazi.

Even the top Nazis of the 'inner guard' were not immune from his system of control, for when they became too powerful or were seen by him as a challenge, he acted accordingly. Thus, Göring was denied access to Hitler's person and ignored in policy discussions after 1941; Goebbels was 'cold-shouldered' in the good years until Hitler needed him again in 1942; while Heydrich was sent to Prague. In the last few hours of his life, when he was dictating his will and political testament to his secretary Bormann, Hitler continued to exercise his control. Both Himmler and Göring were 'punished' for their disloyalty and expelled from the Party, losing all their rights. The succession was given to Admiral Dönitz, who was President of the Reich and Supreme Commander of the Armed Forces.

The personal feuding and scrambling for office which was the inevitable consequence of such a personal system did not greatly bother Hitler. At times he seemed to have encouraged it, as with Göring against Röhm, and Goebbels and Himmler and Bormann against Heydrich. Such rivalries enhanced his own position as supreme arbiter. Hitler was concerned to prevent the rapid rise of anyone who might try to challenge his leadership, as in the case of Heydrich. Hess was appointed 'deputy to the Führer' because he represented no danger to Hitler. Hitler had a neurotic suspicion of opposition; not surprisingly, given the endless intrigues which went on around his person. He was prepared to act violently to deal with such a threat and demonstrated on many occasions that not even the top Nazi leaders, 'friends' and long-time associates could rely on his unwavering and consistent support.

## What was Hitler's role in policy-making?

There is now a consensus of opinion that between 1933 and 1941 Hitler was central to the regime and that certain developments would not have happened without his authority:

- The SS would not have developed on the scale that it did, so that it eventually threatened to take over the State.
- Extermination of the Jews would not have happened, though there would have been discrimination and racial laws.
- Germany would not have been involved in a general war in 1939 since there is evidence that war, as a policy, was unpopular with the people, the Army and high-ranking Nazis such as Göring.

One recent historian of the Third Reich, Ian Kershaw, has claimed that as Führer Hitler had three important functions to perform: to integrate the many different and antagonistic groups; to mobilise the actions of his subordinates; to legalise many of the barbaric actions taken by subordinates. Many of those in authority believed that it was their duty to comply with Hitler and what he wished in terms of ideology and policy. This often implied what they thought Hitler wanted, which meant that he did not always have to give direct instructions.

Hitler's decision-making role was crucial in four important areas.

### Collapse of the international order

Hitler seized the opportunity in the 1930s as European diplomacy collapsed. Hitler took the big decisions in foreign policy, but these were in tune with the times. He exploited the weaknesses of his opponents and he was central to the collapse of international order as a result of the unreliability of his promises.

### Growth of an ideological executive force in Germany

By 1936 the amalgamation of the NSDAP with the SS and state organisation of the police had been achieved. This centralised organisation policed the state, while the SS interpreted the Führer's wishes and policed ideology. After the 1938 *Anschluss*, which incorporated Austria into Germany, Jews were expelled from Vienna. This process continued as other countries were absorbed.

### Disintegration of the ordered state

Hitler stood aloof from the intrigues of different power groups. He was a non-interventionist dictator which linked closely with his ***Social Darwinist*** ideas, his personal habits and his rare appearances. He rarely read government official papers. By 1938 no central government was left, the cabinet did not meet during the war years while Hitler was away on the eastern front and in his various 'wolf's lairs' in Prussia. Goebbels spoke of a leadership and government crisis.

### Key Term

**Social Darwinism** was a social and political philosophy derived from a distorted version of Charles Darwin's views of natural selection through survival of the fittest. Hitler's personal philosophy was based on the idea that struggle was a permanent feature of life and only the strong survived. He believed that the modern state, instead of devoting itself to protecting the weak, should reject its inferior population in favour of the strong and healthy. This idea became the theme of most of his speeches: victory goes to the strong and the weak must be eliminated. It was the ideology behind his subsequent policies to kill the mentally and physically handicapped and the Jews. He was hostile to any religion or ideology which put emphasis on the rights of the weak or the poor – such as Christianity or socialism – since this would distort the natural processes through which the stronger and healthier race would always prevail.

### The dropping of civilised restraints

This was an important area of Hitler's personal influence. The compulsory sterilisation programme of those with a mental and/or physical handicap was approved by Hitler in July 1933. It grew out of a concern over falling birth rates and male losses during the First World War. Programmes of selective breeding of humans occurred elsewhere in Europe, but in Germany there was a drastic difference in terms of the categories of people chosen and numbers (320,000–350,000 between 1934 and 1945). In 1938 this progressed on to the euthanasia programme which was a compulsory killing of handicapped children in institutional homes. It was extended, with the outbreak of war, to include sick adults. Whether it was due to the pressure of public protest or to the fact that Hitler had achieved his objective of making space in hospitals for war casualties, the programme was abandoned in 1941 though not before 72,000 people had been killed. It continued secretly in concentration camps between 1941 and 1943 when a further 30,000 to 50,000 died.

Hitler was also responsible for the radicalisation of the policy against Jews from November 1938, though it was Goebbels who worked to achieve Hitler's goals. Hitler distanced himself because the policy was unattractive even in Nazi circles. From 1940 onwards Himmler and his deputy, Heydrich, took the initiative to extend the policy first to Poland and then, in the summer of 1941, to Russia. Hitler sanctioned their actions. Thus the 'final solution' came into being as an accumulation of local initiatives. Hitler's role was to legitimise different groups' attempts to implement his wishes. His role was as a 'figurehead', incorporating the four important policy areas of the Führer.

Hitler, then, was central to the policies of war and genocide. Had he died, or been removed, the regime would have collapsed because Hitler integrated the divergent Nazi groups. The succession would ultimately have passed to the Army who had no love for an over-extended war or expansion into the east.

# TASKS

**1 Make notes on the following themes using the questions as a focus:**

**Hitler's role within the NSDAP**

**a** How, and in what ways, was Hitler able to dominate the NSDAP so that in the view of one of his biographers, J. C. Fest, 'what we call National Socialism is inconceivable without his person'?

**b** Who composed Hitler's

i 'personal entourage'

ii 'kitchen cabinet'

iii 'personal staff'

iv 'old Munich friends'?

**Hitler's role in policy-making**

**d** In what respects can Hitler be described as a 'man of extraordinary characteristics'?

**e** What was Hitler's role in policy-making?

**f** To what extent was Hitler in control of policy-making?

**2 Classroom task – a debate**

This class considers the motion that

*'Hitler, far from being master in the Third Reich, was a weak dictator'.*

This debate is concerned with structures of power. It centres on the extent to which Hitler was a 'prisoner' of forces outside of his control. The main arguments of intentionalists and structuralists are relevant to the debate.

Divide the class into two; one side to argue for the motion and the other side to argue against. To debate the motion effectively you will need to investigate the following points:

- Decision-making – was Hitler weak in the sense that he regularly avoided making decisions? Was he weak because his decisions were altered by others?
- State of government
- Hitler's relationships with others
- Extent of Hitler's control over the state/freedom of action
- What conclusions can be drawn?

CHAPTER THREE

# WAS HITLER CONSISTENT IN HIS IDEAS?

## Objectives

- **To understand the relationship between Hitler's ideas and the policies of the regime**
- **To understand the extent to which Hitler's aims represented a continuity with those of his predecessors.**

**Profile** ADOLF HITLER 1889–1945

*Hitler thought of himself as a German, though he was born in Austria, in a town called Braunau-am-Inn. He failed at school and in two attempts to gain entrance to the Academy of Fine Arts in Vienna in 1907 and 1908. For the next five years he lived on the streets of Vienna and in a home for destitute men. In May 1913 he moved to Munich in Bavaria, possibly to avoid registering for military service. However, when war broke out in August 1914, he enlisted as a volunteer in the 16th Bavarian Reserve Infantry Regiment and spent four years on the Western Front. Though he never rose above the rank of corporal, he did win the Iron Cross for bravery.*

*The defeat of 1918 was traumatic for Hitler and he drew the conclusion that his country had been betrayed. While still a soldier he joined the German Workers' Party (DAP) in September 1919. He soon took it over, renamed it the National Socialist German Workers' Party (NSDAP) and provided it with a 25-point programme. Hitler had a talent for public speaking and by 1933 he was the leading personality among the nationalist parties of Bavaria. In 8 November 1923 he led an unsuccessful attempt to seize power in Munich. He was arrested and sentenced to five years' imprisonment in Landsberg prison. Though he only served nine months he used the time well, dictating his political autobiography* Mein Kampf *to Rudolf Hess.*

*Hitler always spoke of possessing a basic philosophy which had evolved over the years in the light of his experiences as a down-and-out, in the First World War and in the difficult times which beset Germany under Weimar. During his Vienna years he developed his ideals (*weltanschauung*) which became the driving forces in his life. These forces consisted of a fanatical nationalism, a hatred for Jews and Marxism and a conviction that Fate had* *chosen him to do great things. Although historians differ about the importance of* Mein Kampf *to an understanding of Hitler's subsequent policies, it remains a vital source for understanding his basic mind and beliefs.*

# Was Hitler consistent in his ideas?

Hitler's view, stated in *Mein Kampf* ('My Struggle'), was that all propaganda must be presented in a popular form. Add to this the Nazi belief that adherence to the Party should be based more on faith and obedience than rational thought and it is easy to see how a Nazi leader, Hans Frank, could write as early as 1924, 'our programme, in two words, reads "Adolf Hitler"', or how Göring could state in 1934, 'the programme reads "Germany"'. In fact, the leading writer of National Socialist ideology was not Hitler, but Alfred Rosenberg. He wrote a number of anti-semitic pamphlets, and re-issued a nineteenth-century pamphlet entitled 'The Protocols of the Elders of Zion'. This claimed to describe a Jewish plot to achieve world domination, was later identified as a forgery, but was accepted by Hitler. In 1925 Rosenberg published his work, *The Myth of the Twentieth Century* which was regarded as a National Socialist bible for its racial theories. In 1934 he was made responsible for training Nazi party members in National Socialist ideology.

In these circumstances it is not surprising for people at the time, and for many historians and commentators since, to doubt whether Hitler really had a coherent ideology. One commentator, William Shirer, has gone so far as to describe Hitler's ideology as 'a grotesque hodge-podge concocted by a half-baked, uneducated neurotic' – a view not shared by all historians. Alan Bullock, a foremost expert on Hitler, believes that 'Hitler showed considerable consistency in adhering to certain ideas and conceptions throughout 25 years of political activity'.

## Main themes in Hitler's ideology

### The German *völk* and the need for racial purity

Hitler had a strong sense of community and nationalism. He stressed the need for all people of the same blood to be incorporated into the same Reich or *völk*. This included those Germans who had been forced to live within the frontiers of neighbouring countries because of territorial changes imposed in the Treaty of Versailles. This policy, known as pan-Germanism, was the positive part of his racial policy and one of the earliest features of his political thinking. Hitler wrote that Austria must be restored to the great Germanic motherland regardless of economic considerations. He detested the Slav races of Eastern Europe and the mixing of other racial elements with Germans.

## Source

*Blood mixture and the resultant drop in the racial level is the sole cause of the dying out of old cultures; for men do not perish as a result of lost wars, but by the loss of that force of resistance which is contained only in pure blood. All who are not of good race in this world are chaff. And all occurrences in world history are only expression of the races' instinct for self-preservation...*

*What we must fight for is to safeguard the existence and reproduction of our race and our people, the sustenance of our children and the purity of our blood, the freedom and independence of the fatherland, so that our people may mature for the fulfilment of the mission allotted it by the creator of the universe.*

*Those who are physically and mentally unhealthy and unworthy must not perpetuate their suffering in the body of their children.*

*Adolf Hitler* ***Mein Kampf****, translated by Ralph Manheim (1969)*

Hitler emphasised the consolidation of 'pure' elements within the community (*gemeinschaft*) and the need to encourage racial attitudes. He talked of a new social order, a *völksgemeinschaft* (people's community), which would be based on the peasantry. Racially, he considered them to be the purest elements of the *völk* and he believed that they represented the traditional values which had been lost in urban society. This *völksgemeinschaft* was at the heart of Hitler's social revolution, for belonging to this community would become more important than belonging to a particular sector of society. Although Nazi support for the peasantry has been described as one of the few consistent principles of Nazi life, it failed because of the contradictions in Hitler's goals. His plans to recover lost German lands and people required rearmament and this conflicted with the preservation of a pre-industrial peasant class.

This desire to incorporate all Germans into the Reich represented one of Hitler's continuous links both with his imperial predecessors and the nineteenth-century German philosopher, Fichte. Hitler was entirely won over by the success of the great imperial statesman, Bismarck, in creating a united Reich and laying the foundations of a mighty Germany. He approved of Bismarck's policy of 'blood and iron', of struggle and battle. Nazi thinking had a strong sense of Germany's past, which encouraged a nationalist spirit, while also giving Nazism an aura of tradition. Perhaps it is not surprising that some historians have seen Hitler's foreign policy as a continuity with that of his predecessors and of the professional diplomats at the Foreign Ministry. It was aimed at making Germany the greatest power in Europe. Fichte had given a great impulse to such national feeling and saw in the purity of the language an indication of a healthy nation. He emphasised the *völk* and believed in expansion and domination.

However, where Hitler differed from his predecessors was in the scope of his territorial ambitions. He believed that his ambition for dominant power status in Europe could not be realised within the frontiers of Imperial, much less Weimar, Germany. He was not interested in merely confining himself to a recovery of the 1914 frontiers, which was the goal of the traditional elites and the Army. Hitler's goal for National Socialism was an abandonment of the foreign policy of the prewar period which he regarded as 'senseless' and 'feeble'. He dismissed Germany's 1914 frontiers as 'political absurdity', 'anything but logical, neither complete nor sensible', and the 'results of chance'. The struggle for living space, not the improvement of existing political frontiers, would determine the nature of the foreign policy of the National Socialist state. (You might find it helpful to study the timeline and map 1 in Part One. Note the extent to which Hitler remained consistent to this aspect of his ideology and succeeded in incorporating people of the same blood into the same Reich or *völk*.)

### Source

*We stop the endless German movement to the south and west, and turn our gaze towards the land in the east.*

*Adolf Hitler* ***Mein Kampf****, translated by Ralph Manheim (1969)*

### Racial superiority of the Aryans

Closely related to his ideal of the need for racial purity was Hitler's concept of the racial superiority of the Aryans (see Figure 11). This is an area of his ideology which was confused and contradictory because the existence of an Aryan race was a myth. It existed only in the writings of nineteenth-century philosophers who used the term to include all those Scandinavian and Northern people who could be described as 'Nordic'. Hitler further confined the term to the Germans whom he saw as a master-race or *Herrenvölk*. He believed that the perfection and purity of the Aryan race should be preserved through the elimination of those who were mentally or physically handicapped. As you read in chapter 2, his attempt to implement this through his policy of sterilisation and euthanasia had to be officially abandoned in the face of public hostility. However, it was continued in the concentration camps.

Hitler's racial ideas were not new, but drew upon nineteenth-century race theories associated with the writings of GOBINEAU and HOUSTON STEWART CHAMBERLAIN.

**Profiles** GOBINEAU

*A nineteenth-century French racial theorist who saw humankind as being in the process of decline. Race provided the key to history and civilisation. Gobineau distinguished three basic races: black, white and yellow and set out to show the superiority of the whites. Racial mixture would lead to the ruin of the white race of which the Aryans were the finest branch. He claimed no true civilisation had existed in Europe except where the Aryans were dominant for they were superior in intelligence and energy. Gobineau singled out the German race for special mention. The last remnants of the Aryan race were to be found in North-West Europe, though he did not view the modern Aryan in a narrowly German sense.*

HOUSTON STEWART CHAMBERLAIN

*A British-born writer who had great influence in Germany. He thought race the most important factor in historical development. Chamberlain saw the Jews as an alien people. He used the term 'Teutonic peoples' to mean the different North European races.*

Insistence on race was one of Hitler's most fundamental beliefs. Race bound Germans together in their belief that they were superior and had the right to subjugate inferior peoples and treat them as slaves. It was this belief which led to the abuse of concentration camp slave

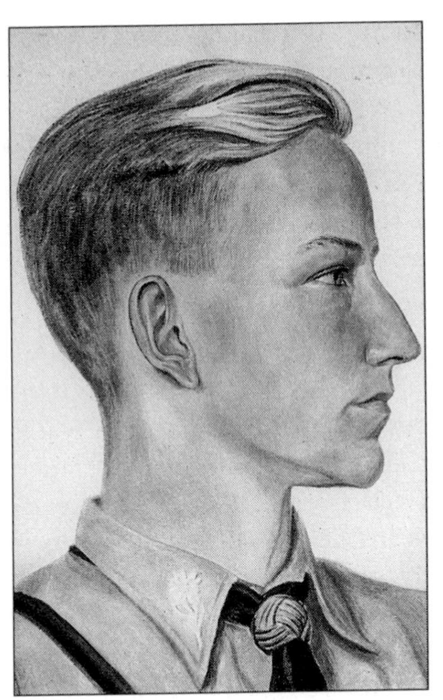

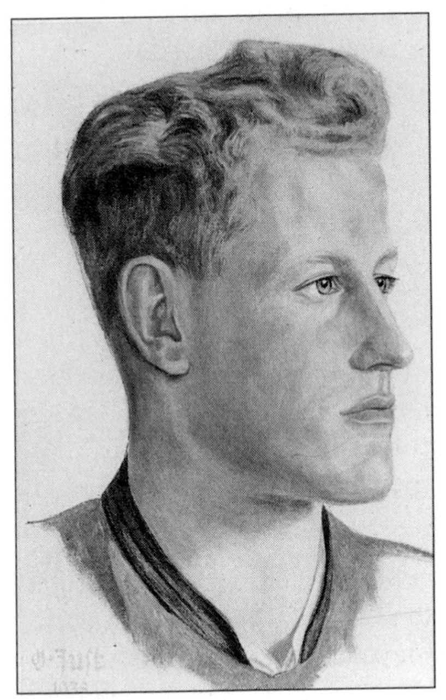

**Figure 11** Examples of 'ideal Aryan physiognomies' painted by Oskar Just and Wolfgang Willrich

labour. In fact, although Hitler talked as if the whole German nation were Aryan, his real view was rather different. His Aryans were the elite of the Nazi Party and later the SS and it was for this reason that they had the right to rule over the German people. This explains why Hitler could refer to the Nazi seizure of power as a 'racial' revolution because it represented the replacement of one ruling caste by another.

**Anti-semitism**

Removal of the Jews and the influence of Jewry were at the core of Hitler's system of beliefs and it became the central motivation of his policies. When he acquired these ideas is uncertain. Possible dates suggested are during Hitler's down-and-out days in Vienna or defeat in 1918, or the subsequent Treaty of Versailles or later. A recent biographer of Hitler, Ian Kershaw, prefers the earlier date (the Vienna years), while the effect of war and the 'stab in the back' reaction cemented these ideas from September 1919 onwards. The early 1920s' speeches contain reference to Hitler's anti-semitism, but they were no different from the *völkisch* tradition of Germany in the nineteenth and early twentieth centuries. Hitler blamed the Jews for being a part of those responsible for German collapse at the end of the 1914–18 war and part of a Jewish–Marxist plot to dominate the world.

However, there was an apparent inconsistency between Hitler's anti-semitism and his actions. Anti-semitism did not figure prominently in Nazi propaganda during the 1920s. As early as 1924 the Press commented on the little reference to anti-semitism in Hitler's anti-Marxist speeches, but the shift was a tactical move. Hitler recognised that the German people were largely indifferent to the Jewish question. Despite this apparent inconsistency, there was no change in policy direction. There was always a general aim to get rid of them. Prior to the outbreak of war, the regime confined its anti-semitic policies to depriving Jews of their civil liberties and encouraging them to emigrate. After 1941 the policy changed, especially with the failure of the Madagascar Plan in 1940 (see timeline on page 3).

In 1941 Rosenberg was appointed Reich Minister for the Eastern Occupied Territories and promoted the Germanisation of eastern peoples under brutal conditions, supervised camp labour, rounded up workers for work in Germany and arranged for the extermination of the Jews.

## Conquest of *lebensraum* in the East and hostility to Russia

Hitler made constant references in *Mein Kampf* to his concern with the desperate urgency of Germany's territorial requirements. He was concerned with its small size compared with the other European powers and concluded that Germany was not a world power. He believed that the real threat to Germany's existence lay in the East, whose peoples could, with their unlimited numbers, overrun the insignificant area to which Germany had been restricted by the Treaty of Versailles. Hitler regarded hostility to Marxism/Bolshevism as a crusade, even though Russia offered no threat in the 1920s and 1930s. Nevertheless, he believed that German security could only be met by the possession of more land. He was hostile to any suggestion that Germany's population growth should be restricted, but the problem of food supply had to be met. He was opposed to a reliance on foreign imports and argued that real economic security could only be achieved by ensuring that a people could feed itself. Since it would be impossible to adapt the fertility of the soil to the increasing population, then the German *völk* had to secure its living space at the expense of others.

Hitler's decisive argument in favour of territorial expansion was the disastrous effect of a territorial deficiency on Germany's military position. It was not only a question of inadequate manpower because strategic security was also directly dependent on territorial size. His fear was that the area of the German Reich would 'vanish completely', compared with that of other world powers. He feared that Germany would sink into insignificance because it was no longer a world power. Hitler considered that the best solution lay in the acquisition of more land to meet both its economic and strategic needs.

The conquest of land in the East was not sufficient. The only way of making German domination permanent was to remove the native population and settle German farmers on the rich soil of the Ukraine (a policy of 'Germanisation'). He realised that these plans meant war with Russia, a change in Germany's alliance partners and an aggressive and ruthless policy directed against the Jews whom he believed were aiming at world domination. Hitler's racism and anti-semitism came together in his plans to protect the Aryan race/German people through territorial expansion at the expense of weaker and inferior peoples.

Hitler had been influenced by a contemporary academic, ***Karl Haushofer***, who popularised the ***geopolitics*** current among a group of academics at Munich University. Their grand schemes for the subjugation of Slav peoples supplied Hitler with a scientific explanation for racial prejudice. From the geopoliticians he learnt to appreciate the strategic advantages of expansion, that in the air age the military defence of states would depend on their physical size.

## KEY TERM

**Geopolitics** was a social science drawing on geography, politics, strategy and related disciplines. Concepts such as *lebensraum* (living space) could be said to be geopolitical in nature. The chief protagonist of this approach in Germany was **Karl Haushofer** (1869–1946), a professor at Munich University. Geopolitics, as promoted by Haushofer, formed an ideological link between traditional German expansionism and the more radical racist doctrines of National Socialism.

Hitler's preoccupation with living space did not appear to be consistent. Between 1930 and 1933 little was said about *lebensraum*; he was concerned with attacks on the Weimar Republic, unemployment and revision of the terms of the Treaty of Versailles. The non-aggression pact which the regime signed with Russia in 1939 suggested a further turning away from his ideology. But Hitler was buying time; he wanted to complete his plans to acquire territory at Poland's expense and wait for the opportune moment to move against Russia, which he did in 1941.

### Power of the State and the Führer principle

Hitler had little faith in parliamentary democracy which he regarded as alien to German tradition. He saw it as idealistic, weak and liable to encourage Communism.

Hitler believed it was the task of National Socialism to purge Germany of this alien influence, which he did during the period 1933–4. Instead of democracy, he proposed the *Führerprinzip* (leadership principle), for only a determined leader could oppose Marxism and democracy. Propaganda would be used to appeal to people's emotions. Hitler hoped to destroy socialist ideas. As far as the *Führerprinzip* was concerned the will of the nation was demonstrated in the person of Hitler, who was independent of all groups and interests. He symbolised the political unity of the people in opposition to individual interests.

Hitler thought that the rights of the individual should be of secondary importance when they clashed with the interests of the community or the State. These rights would be surrendered, but people would be compensated by social reform to remove grievances. Hitler was brought into contact with socialist ideas in his attacks against the Marxists and Social Democrats whom he condemned for their international character. He recognised that the masses could be dominated by a nationalist movement so long as it did not neglect social problems. Marxism was to be countered by a ruthless programme of social reform and an attack on the social failings of the Kaiser's Germany.

Hitler was reluctant to acknowledge his indebtedness to others, but it is possible to identify some nineteenth-century German intellectual roots to his ideas on the State and the submissiveness of the individual:

| Philosopher | Intellectual roots to Hitler's ideas |
| --- | --- |
| Hegel<br>A professor of philosophy and a Prussian nationalist who glorified the State. His ideas were influential in German society. | He contributed to ideas about nationalist power, the doctrine of State supremacy and of war as its necessary instrument. |
| Treitschke<br>A German professor of history who glorified the State and the necessity for war. | He was the author of *Politik*; the keynote of his thought was the State as a power which would be hard and harsh so that the individual had to sacrifice himself to service in the State. |

## A philosophy of life

Hitler's ideology was formed from theories current in the twentieth century. This is true of his philosophy of life which he called his *weltanschauung*. At the heart of this was the concept of struggle which represented a crude form of 'Social Darwinism' (see key term, page 55). 'Struggle' appeared often in his speeches, as did the claims that 'man has become great through struggle' and 'the first fundamental of any rational *weltanschauung* is the fact that . . . force alone is decisive'. Hitler regarded struggle as the basis of all achievement for 'only through struggle has man raised himself above the animal world'.

| Philosopher | Intellectual roots to Hitler's ideas |
|---|---|
| **Treitschke**<br>His lectures at Berlin University in 1874 had an important influence over the youth of the new Germany and influenced the future. His ideas became characteristic of German thought and were later to appear with dynamic effect among the Nazis. | He provided a theoretical basis for the ***'Prussianisation'*** of Germany. He glorified war and saw it as of permanent importance in the policy of the State, while arbitration was denounced. He believed that war was both justifiable and moral, while the ideal of perpetual peace was not only impossible but immoral as well. |
| **Nietzsche**<br>The Nazis made him one of the philosophical supports of their way of life. | He stressed the importance of force and was obsessed with power and aristocratic leadership. He stressed the importance to society of the creation of a vigorous elite of ruthless leaders under a superman. The latter would exercise unlimited power with no moral restraint. In some ways, he stood outside the characteristic lines of German nationalist thought. He was not racist or anti-semitic. |

### KEY TERM

**Prussianisation** – Prussia (identified in Figure 2) was a remote frontier state with a long military history based on conquest of surrounding lands. Its ruling aristocracy were the landowning Junkers who owned large estates which gave them control over the peasantry. Prussia took a leading role in the unification of Germany in 1871– 90, providing the core of the German army, its leading statesman, Bismarck, and its king who became Emperor of Germany. In the view of the American commentator, William Shirer, Prussianism permeated all Germany; through its ruling class who controlled the Army and the bureaucracy, and who were anti-democratic, anti-liberal and pro-militarist. According to some historians, German militarism was important to Hitler's success.

However, his concept of struggle was only one of three fundamental principles which Hitler believed controlled the existence of every nation; the other two were purity of blood and the resourcefulness of the individual. These three principles also provide the key to Hitler's contempt of other people's beliefs. He criticised those who put internationalism before race; democracy before the rule of a great leader; individuality before inequality and valued peace above struggle.

## Extent to which Hitler's ideology clashed with political realities

The political reality in Germany in January 1933 was that Hitler had been 'handed' the chancellorship by the elites. However, as we saw in Part One, he had important restraints on his freedom of action until the changes of 1938. He was caught between the conflicting demands of the left wing of his party and the wishes of the elite. If he was to retain the support of the elite, Hitler would have to compromise some aspects of ideology to make some concessions to the Right. He needed the support of the Army for his long-term foreign policy goals, and of the elite who were still in control of the Establishment – the judiciary, civil service and bureaucracy. These compromises involved a surrender of those ideals of social reform which had promised a new world to many. They give added weight to those who have charged Hitler's ideology with inconsistency.

The extent to which ideology clashed with political realities in 1933–4 can best be summarised as follows:

| Ideology | Continuity and change in the face of political realities |
|---|---|
| Nationalism<br>(*i.e.* re-creation of German greatness and Empire) | Strong resentment was felt by Germans against the Treaty of Versailles. Hitler owed much of his success to defeat in war and the shame of Versailles. |
| Military power<br>Pan-Germanism<br>(*i.e.* the recovery of lands and people lost in 1919) | Hitler did not change his territorial ambitions. |

| | |
|---|---|
| Anti-Marxism | The fear of 1929–33 was that a left-wing government would succeed in Germany, a fear reinforced by the success of the KPD in Weimar elections. Hitler's hostility was shared by all social groups apart from the workers, and this helped him come to power. The elites and the middle class saw Hitler as the best alternative to a Marxist government.<br><br>**Hitler did not change his anti-Marxist stance.** |
| Racist and anti-semitic | The people were indifferent to anti-semitism though there was some resentment felt, especially by the middle class, against the Jews who were seen as the 'scapegoats' for the runaway inflation of 1929– 33.<br><br>**Hitler's policies appeared confused and contradictory, but in reality there was no fundamental change in intent only in tactics as circumstances changed.** |
| State, leader and Party | There were strong anti-parliamentary and anti-democratic feelings because Weimar was identified with the hated Versailles settlement and the failure to protect people against the 1923 and 1929 economic crises. Parliamentary democracy had already given way to rule by presidential decree under Article 48 of the Constitution. There was no clash between Hitler, Nazi ideology and political realities of 1933.<br><br>**There was a general acceptance that Weimar must go.**<br><br>The clash arose over what would replace Weimar – would it be the elites, the Army and the bureaucracy, or would it be the Nazi Party. The elites of Weimar handed power to Hitler because of his appeal to the masses, to the nationalists and the fact that he was the only viable alternative to the KPD. They supported his return to strong authoritarian government provided they |

| | |
|---|---|
| | preserved their role and prestige within the State. Hitler recognised the importance of placating the powerful elites of the bureaucracy and army of Weimar.<br><br>**He continued to work with the elites until 1938 when his regime took a new direction.** |
| Role of the State (*e.g.* social reform to turn people away from Communism) | Improvement in people's conditions and promise of deliverance from economic constraints clashed with revitalising German power and greatness which needed the support of the industrial elites. The wealthy landowners, the Junkers, were opposed to land reform and they dominated the bureaucracy and the army whose support Hitler required if he was to achieve his foreign policy objectives. Röhm and the SA pressed for radical social reform.<br><br>**Hitler compromised in favour of the elites and abandoned the left-wing programme of the Party.** |
| Social Darwinism | Struggle was at the heart of Hitler's beliefs, but people looked for an end to the violence of 1929–33 and to the danger of the SA. Economic and political realities clashed with Nazi philosophy of establishing new Party-dominated structures. The violence of Party ideology and the actions of the SA clashed with the need for 'legality'. The promise of a new world achieved through revolution had to be contained.<br><br>**Hitler abandoned the social revolutionary part of Party ideology.** |

Early writers viewed Hitler as a cynical opportunist lacking firm convictions whose ideology was confused and contradictory. More recent writings have stressed Hitler's skilful marriage of his philosophy of life with tactics to exploit people and situations to his best advantage. Although much of his ideology was not new, he gave it such an intensity that under him it became revolutionary.

## TASKS

**Individual work – essay planning**

Most essays call for analysis, comparison or evaluation. All essays will require some description and possibly narrative, but what is usually required at A Level is argument. Your task is to plan an answer to the following question:

*'What was the nature of Nazi ideology at the time that Hitler came to power, and to what extent did this ideology conflict with political realities during 1933–4?'*

Note that this question is in two parts: the first part is representative of *list* type questions which are of a descriptive and analytical type. List questions normally start with the command: 'Why', 'Account for', 'What', 'With what results', 'For what reasons', 'Explain'. Such questions may require an investigation of causes, effects and consequences and where there are several causes it is helpful to classify them either under political, economical, social and religious, or as short-term, intermediate-term, long-term factors, or major and minor factors to indicate priority. In the above question you would be expected to describe the main features of Nazi ideology and evaluate what these amounted to in practice.

The second part is a *significance* question. Significance questions normally start with: 'How far', 'How important', 'How effectively', 'How valuable', 'To what extent', 'What was the role of'. This type of question requires you to decide upon the relative importance of factors. All such questions require analysis, evaluation and historical judgement. Taking the question above as an example, you would be required to select those aspects of Nazi ideology which met with hostility and required change, as against those which were acceptable and were continued. You would be expected to refer to all the significant factors that must be investigated to reach a balanced conclusion. It is important to indicate which factors are significant in terms of conflict, such as the left-wing call for a social revolution, and which factors are less significant and did not conflict, such as Nazi belief in a strong nationalist and authoritarian government.

# DID HITLER'S REGIME ACHIEVE AN ECONOMIC MIRACLE?

## Objectives

- To evaluate and interpret primary source material by understanding and extracting information from it and reaching conclusions
- To understand the extent to which the regime succeeded in solving Germany's economic problems
- To understand the motives which lay behind economic recovery.

## Germany's economic condition in 1933

When Hitler became chancellor in January 1933 he accepted responsibility for a depressed economy which had all the effects of a social catastrophe. The decline in world trade affected German industry although the economy was already in recession in 1928. German investors moved their money to safer havens in Europe which meant that there was an outflow of German-based investment; factories closed, industrial production fell along with national income. At the height of the depression the textbooks state that the number of registered unemployed reached 6 million but recent research has shown this figure to be closer to 8.5 million. The latter figure represents the number of unemployed who were removed from the register by the government by 1932 through its programme of voluntary labour service, different kinds of welfare funding or because they were female.

Even those who remained in employment suffered. There was widespread reduction in the number of hours worked from 7.5 to 6 hours on average a day which meant declining earnings. Small businesses and shops suffered a decline in income as consumer demand fell. This was a catastrophe for the owners of small businesses because they had no reserves. Many businesses and even some banks went bankrupt – on average 10,000 a year between 1929 and 1933. Many of the middle class suffered and had to rely on soup kitchens because welfare favoured the factory worker. There was a shortage of gold and foreign exchange reserves which prevented the purchase of overseas technology, raw materials and foodstuffs. The scale of this economic catastrophe cut across most groups in society.

## Hitler's attitude to Germany's economic problems

No coherent plan had emerged before January 1933 and Hitler did not turn his direct attention to the economy until May 1933 after he had secured his position. He had no interest in economics. For him it was merely a means to achieve his political and military ends. The regime adopted three approaches to solve the problems of the economy:

1. A policy of self-sufficiency (autarky) achieved through the creation of a trading community under German dominance
2. Deficit financing – spending money on public works to create jobs which would stimulate market demand.
3. A defence economy (*wehrwirtschaft*) whereby Germany's peacetime economy was geared to the demands of total war.

However, the old view that economic planning was confused and a prey to competing arguments by groups has given way to a belief that it was more coherent and consistent than concentration on Hitler or Göring might suggest. This does not mean that it could not also be opportunist. In the early years of the regime, policies tended to evolve out of the demands of the situation rather than being the result of careful planning. No single unified economic system prevailed though, according to some leading historians, Hitler adopted a political, rather than an economic, view of economic problems.

Displaying his Social Darwinist philosophy, Hitler believed that a solution to Germany's economic problems was a 'matter of will'. Hitler believed that other countries of Europe were opposed to Germany's recovery. He wanted to unite the people in a people's community under Nazi leadership. Germans would have to abandon class, economic and religious differences and become one people dedicated to the needs of the state. Everyone had to work hard and to make sacrifices to restore Germany's greatness. Hitler blamed Germany's problems on the mistakes of the various democratic governments of the Weimar Republic, rather than on changes in the pattern of world trade.

Early Nazi manifestos had tended to be anti-capitalist, but political realities required that Hitler's economic policy frequently had to compromise between a number of competing, often contradictory and even hostile forces, to satisfy the different economic interest groups:

- He was committed to save the *mittelstand* (middle class), to improve the lot of the farmer and the peasants and to revive business fortunes.
- He wished to rearm Germany rapidly and to develop a self-sufficient economy, but he could not politically afford to introduce rationing or sacrifice the standard of living of the working classes.
- He was pledged to reduce unemployment and to achieve this he was prepared to spend public money to stimulate the economy. However, he was concerned to control inflation.

Hitler was willing to ally with the leaders of big business because he needed them to restore confidence and prosperity (see profile of HJALMAR SCHACHT). It was not until the end of 1937, when the economy had been revived, that control passed to more radical Nazis.

**Profile** HJALMAR SCHACHT 1877–1979

*The son of Danish parents who emigrated to the United States, only to return to Germany, he made his career in banking. In 1919 he helped found the German Democratic Party (DDP). A fervent nationalist, he was hostile to the amount of money Germany was expected to pay the allies as reparations (compensation for war damage). He was very ambitious and progressed through banking circles. In 1930, having read* Mein Kampf, *he decided that Hitler was a political genius who might save Germany by supporting a sound economy in a strong state. He left the DDP and became a supporter, though never a member, of the Nazi Party. He helped Hitler secure financial support from the rich Rhineland industrialists from 1930 onwards. He supported Hitler's cause in the prolonged negotiations which preceded the Nazi rise to political power in 1932–3. Hitler rewarded him in March 1933 by making him President of the Reichsbank, a post he held until 1939. This was followed by his appointment as Reich Minister of Economics, from August 1934 to November 1937 when he resigned in protest at Göring's policies under the second Four Year Plan. His appointment reflected the need of the Nazi leadership to work with the powerful forces of big business, for Schacht was a respected international banker and a man of great ability.*

*By a law of 3 July 1934 Schacht was given dictatorial powers over the economy and he contributed as much as Hitler to the construction of the Third Reich. His approach to the problems of high unemployment and depression was influenced by the economist, John Maynard Keynes. He advocated a policy of state intervention in the economy through public works schemes which would encourage employment and consumer demand. Schacht was also the economic expert behind German rearmament, using the financial facilities of the Reichsbank to their fullest extent.*

### Source 1

*As long as I remained in office, whether at the Reichsbank or the Ministry of Economics, Hitler never interfered with my work. He never attempted to give me any instructions, but let me carry out my own ideas in my own way and without criticism... However, when he realised that the moderation of my financial policy was a stumbling block in his reckless plans (*in foreign policy*), he began, with Göring's connivance, to go behind my back and counter my arrangements.*

*Hjalmar Schacht* ***Account Settled*** *(1949)*

# Economic policies to achieve recovery

## 1933–6

In this period Hitler's economic policies were not new. He continued with his predecessors' policies, applying public/government spending into creating employment, while vigorously controlling prices and wages. These policies were already beginning to have an effect for, by the time Hitler became chancellor, the economy was beginning to come out of depression. Unemployment was past its peak.

### Government controls

Using the powers he was given over the economy in July 1934, Schacht introduced the 'New Plan' of September which provided for control by government of all aspects of trade and currency exchange. In this way, the government set the priorities. Schacht pursued a policy of economic nationalism with the outside world. He refused to pay reparations and negotiated for the generous settlement of international debts, especially with Britain. He introduced government controls on foreign exchange deals. He directed scarce raw materials to 'key' industries which led to a fall in cotton and wool imports and a rise in iron ore exports. He introduced large-scale export subsidies to bring down prices to a competitive level on the world market. He pursued a policy of self-sufficiency, signing bilateral trade treaties with economically weak countries who could provide the producer materials vital to Germany's economic recovery. In return, Germany exported its surpluses rather than paying cash which meant a system of barter where the value of the mark was negotiated and varied.

### 'Battle for Work'

This was one of several propaganda campaigns launched in the first years. It aimed to restore confidence and to create the impression of 'something being done'. It included the introduction of Labour Service and Emergency Relief Schemes which absorbed a million young people. This was followed by a number of work creation schemes (1933–6), starting with the Law to Reduce Unemployment. This aimed to make the policy of a government-led recovery more effective. Money was poured into public works, such as construction, and subsidies were given for private construction or renovating old buildings. A separate law initiated a large-scale plan for building 7,000 kilometres of motorway which stimulated both employment and subsidiary industries. Income tax rebates and loans were also issued to increase industrial activity in the private sector.

There was also an attempt, by the German Labour Front, to improve working conditions, through its promotion of various organisations – such as the *Kraft durche Freude* ('Strength through Joy') organisation and the *Schonheit der Arbeit* ('Beauty of Work').

### Protection of farming

The regime was also concerned to protect agriculture and the peasantry in the interests of achieving its policy of autarky (self-sufficiency).

A number of policies were introduced designed to protect farmers' markets. Tariffs were imposed on imported foodstuffs while home demand was stimulated for dairy produce. Cheap loans were offered to encourage production and farmers were exempted from tax and from unemployment and health insurance payments. A Reich Food Estate was set up to regulate market prices and to control the distribution of agricultural produce. A Reich Entailment Law was passed to guarantee the future of smaller peasant farmers and smallholders. Under this law, the peasantry was protected from indebtedness and from the land being split up in the course of inheritance. It meant, however, that land could not be sold and younger siblings were dispossessed.

## 1936–9 – the second Four Year Plan

By 1936 Hitler had gone a long way to achieving his primary goal of redeeming his election promises of 'bread and work', a success which secured his position. He now felt confident to progress with his long-terms aims: rearmament and military expansion.

### Secret memo

In 1936 Hitler issued his Secret Memo in which he discussed the 'programme for a final provision of our vital needs'. This is one of the basic documents of the Third Reich and it represents Hitler's response to his critics, such as Schacht and the opposition of German business to all large-scale plans to achieve economic self-sufficiency in the interests of rearmament. The memo, and the second Four Year Plan which it launched, outlined his plans for completely converting the economy and the armed forces for war. Its aim was to make the armed forces and economy ready for war within four years and through a policy of economic self-sufficiency, especially in raw materials, to meet the needs of rearmament. In order to achieve this the Plan highlighted four priorities: increase in agricultural production; retraining of key sectors of the labour force; government regulation of imports and exports; achievement of self-sufficiency in raw materials. Official production goals were set for the production of raw materials.

## Source 2

*The world has been moving with ever-increasing speed towards a new conflict, the most extreme solution of which is Bolshevism . . . I therefore draw up the following programme for a final provision of our vital needs:*

*I Parallel with the military and political rearmament and mobilisation of our nation must go its economic rearmament and mobilisation... In future the interests of individual gentlemen can no longer play any part in these matters. There is only one interest, the interest of the nation; only one view, the bringing of Germany to the point of political and economic self-sufficiency.*

*II ...foreign exchange must be saved in all those areas where our needs can be satisfied by German production...*

*III ...German fuel production must now be stepped up with the utmost speed and brought to final completion within 18 months.*

*IV The mass production of synthetic rubber must also be organised and achieved with the same urgency. From now on there must be no talk of processes not being fully determined and other such excuses... This has nothing whatever to do with the Ministry of Economics. Either we possess today a private industry, in which case its job is to rack its brains about methods of production; or we believe that it is the Government's job to determine methods of production, and in that case we have no further need of private industry.*

*V ...If we really are obliged to build up our domestic economy on autarkic lines, which we are... then the price of raw materials individually considered no longer plays a decisive part.*

*It is further necessary to increase German iron production to the utmost limits... The job of the Ministry of Economics is simply to set the national economic tasks; private industry has to fulfil them. But if private industry thinks itself incapable of doing this, then the National Socialist State will know how to resolve the problem on its own. Nearly four precious years have now gone by... There has been time enough in four years to find out what we cannot do. Now we have to carry out what we can do.*

*I thus set the following tasks:*

*1 The German armed forces must be operational within four years.*

*2 The German economy must be fit for war within four years.*

*Memorandum on the Four Year Plan, August 1936; quoted in J. Noakes and G. Pridham (eds),* ***Nazism 1919 to 1945, A Documentary Reader*** *(1984)*

Such a programme marked an important turning-point in the Nazi regime. From mid 1936 to mid 1937, there was a fierce political struggle among the ruling groups over the course of economic strategy.

**1** There was unanimous agreement among the people, the heads of big business and Hitler's economic experts that there should be recovery in standards of living. They were also prepared to accept moderate rearmament so long as it was not at the expense of consumers and standards of living.

2 Hitler also wanted recovery of standards of living, but then the economy was to supply a massive military machine for a war of revenge for 1918. By 1936 Hitler thought in terms of the economy being directed for rearmament.

This division of purpose was resolved in Hitler's favour. As we saw in Part One, at the end of 1937 and the beginning of 1938 Hitler ended his dependence on the elites. The regime took a new direction and responsibility for the economy was put into the hands of the party faithful. Control over industry became tighter and Schacht found his influence reduced, resigning in 1937. Göring was given responsibility for the second Four Year Plan and he became the real economic dictator. Big business found increasingly that it had to work within the framework laid down by the Nazi leadership. A policy of economic autarky was introduced, designed to make Germany self-sufficient in essential raw materials. This meant building a firm economic block in Central Europe which would provide the resources to wage war.

### Role of rearmament

From 1936 to 1939 rearmament dominated economic growth; exports fell and standards of living were held as growth in the economy was devoted to military spending. There has been considerable debate among historians over the extent of war preparations. The most recent statistics indicate that growth in the economy 1936–9 was devoted to military spending, a feature which contrasts with the view of limited rearmament. R. J. Overy believes that Hitler aimed at total warfare.

However, Hitler recognised the need for a two-stage programme:

1 Germany would be provided with a substructure of war-making capability in the production of steel, iron ore and tools. Between 1936 and 1939, two-thirds of Germany's industrial investment was devoted to this. By the late 1930s Germany produced three times as much steel as Britain, and double the coal.

2 Germany would be provided with a superstructure in the form of weapons. From 1939 Hitler planned that: the German airforce would be increased fivefold; there would be a vast battle fleet; the army would undergo motorisation. But none of these plans were achieved until 1943–5. The cost of this increased so that by 1939 a quarter of the economy was directly committed (see Tables 3 and 4).

**Table 3** Industrial labour forces working on orders for the Armed Forces by 1939

| | 1939 |
|---|---|
| All industry | 21.9% |
| including: | |
| Raw materials | 21.0 |
| Metal manufacture | 28.6 |
| Construction | 30.2 |
| Consumer goods | 12.2 |

Adapted from R.J. Overy, *Mobilisation for total War in Germany 1939–41* (EHR, vol. 103, 1988)

**Table 4** Select statistics comparing German and British war effort by 1939

| Comparison | Germany | Britain |
|---|---|---|
| Index of consumer expenditure (per head) (1938 = 100) | 95.0 | 97.2 |
| Employment in war industries % of all employed | 21.9 | 18.6 |
| % of women in the total of civilian employment | 37.3 | 26.4 |
| % of war expenditure in total national income | 32.2 | 15.0 |

From R. J. Overy, '"Blitzkriegswirtschaft"? Finanzpolitik, Lebensstandard und Arbeitseinsatz in Deutschland 1939–42'. *Vierteljahrshefte für Zeitgeschichte*, vol. 36 (1988)

Standards of living were adversely affected despite the fact that Hitler was keen to maintain a living standard. This involved government control as part of a 'capitalist command economy', which led to the recognition that there were not enough resources. The realisation that there was a mismatch between plans and reality led the regime to solve its problems of scarce resources through a policy of expansion into Central and East Europe – a policy which also accorded with its ideological goals. It gained control of Austria, Czechoslovakia (both 1938) and Poland (1939). This policy provoked growing hostility and opposition from Germany's elite, the army and businessmen who disagreed with Hitler's strategy and its risk to the economy. Hitler had to coerce German capitalism. There was a high element of risk because Germany would not be ready for major war until the mid 1940s. Hitler miscalculated over the Polish crisis and Britain and France declared war before his plans were complete.

# Achievement of an economic miracle: assessment

## Case for

The success of the regime's economic policies has been the subject of much debate. There has been a certain amount of controversy over the reliability of statistics on the Third Reich, especially those relating to the scope and scale of rearmament. The statistics quoted in this chapter represent the results of the most recent research.

### Level of investment

Hitler had placed great emphasis on the need to solve unemployment as a guarantee for political stability. The business community was given a suitable environment for growth, but his hope that private business would create the economic revival was not realised. He had been prepared to rely on the existing experience of business and civil service and had been anxious to avoid appearing to control the economy too closely. Private business did not respond vigorously and the regime became permanently involved in the economy. The regime embarked on a high level of government spending which increased from 17.9 per cent in 1932 to 33.5 per cent in 1938, accelerating after 1936 when the Four Year Plan and a policy of rearmament were launched (see Table 5).

**Table 5** Government spending, 1932–8

| | 1928 | 1932 | 1934 | 1936 | 1938 |
|---|---|---|---|---|---|
| Total expenditure (current prices) [billion RM] | 11.7 | 8.6 | 12.8 | 15.8 | 29.3 |
| Government expenditure as a % of GNP | 14.8% | 17.9% | 22.9% | 22.5% | 35.5% |

Adapted from R. J. Overy, *The Nazi Economic Recovery 1932–8* (Macmillan, 1982)

No one industrial sector on its own was capable of generating the growth which achieved the economic recovery. The statistical evidence in Table 6 suggests that construction and transport had better claims than work-creation or rearmament. Hitler sought to solve the unemployment problem by embarking on a vast new building programme to create an infrastructure which people would associate with the Thousand Year Reich. He hoped that a higher standard of living for all Germans would also follow. However, after 1936 the amount spent on rearmament for a peacetime economy was particularly high. This would require a restructuring of the economy for waging war and a deliberate restraining of consumer expenditure as resources were shifted from consumer to capital goods and industrial raw materials (see Table 7 overleaf). Heavy industry benefited; iron, steel and chemicals, in particular, showed massive growth. The undistributed profits of big business grew from 1.3 to 5 billion RM.

**Table 6** Public expenditure by category 1928–38 [billion RM]

| | 1928 | 1932 | 1934 | 1936 | 1938 |
|---|---|---|---|---|---|
| Total expenditure: | 23.2 | 17.1 | 21.6 | 23.6 | 37.1 |
| Construction | 2.7 | 0.9 | 3.5 | 5.4 | 7.9 |
| Rearmament | 0.7 | 0.7 | 3.0 | 10.2 | 17.2 |
| Transport | 2.6 | 0.8 | 1.8 | 2.4 | 3.8 |
| Work-creation | – | 0.2 | 2.5 | – | – |

Adapted from R. J. Overy, *The Nazi Economic Recovery 1932–8* (Macmillan, 1982)

**Table 7** Relative growth of producer and consumer goods in Germany 1929–38 (1928 = 100)

| | 1929 | 1932 | 1938 |
|---|---|---|---|
| Total production | 10.9 | 58.7 | 124.7 |
| Capital goods | 103.2 | 45.7 | 135.9 |
| Consumer goods | 98.5 | 78.1 | 107.8 |
| Pig-iron | 113.8 | 33.4 | 157.3 |
| Machinery | 103.8 | 40.7 | 147.7 |
| Chemicals | 91.8 | 50.9 | 127.0 |
| Textiles | 92.4 | 79.2 | 107.5 |
| Household furniture | 104.2 | 69.6 | 113.6 |

O. Nathan and M. Fried, ***The Nazi Economic System*** (1944); quoted in R. J. Overy, ***The Nazi Economic Recovery 1932–8*** (Macmillan, 1982)

## Level of employment

The 'Battle for Work' policies were very successful and, combined with an upturn in the trade cycle, they brought the 1929 depression to an end. Unemployment fell rapidly from the 1932 figure of 5.6 million to a labour shortage of 0.4 million by 1938 and great pressure was put on labour (compare Table 8 with the high levels of unemployment shown in chapter 1). This decline in unemployment was an impressive achievement and one which won admiration at home and abroad.

**Table 8** Economic recovery and its impact on (un)employment, 1932–8

| | 1928 | 1932 | 1934 | 1936 | 1938 |
|---|---|---|---|---|---|
| ***GNP*** (1928 prices) [billion RM] | 89.5 | 57.6 | 66.5 | 82.6 | 104.5 |
| Industrial production (1928 = 100) | 100 | 58 | 83 | 107 | 122 |
| Unemployment (in millions) | 1.4 | 5.6 | 2.7 | 1.6 | 0.4 |

Adapted from R. J. Overy, ***The Nazi Economic Recovery 1932–8*** (Macmillan, 1982)

### Key Term

**GNP (Gross National Product)** is an economist's term for the measurement of the total 'value' of the economy. It grew at a remarkably fast rate in Germany during the 1930s and in fact overtook the level achieved by 1928.

### Level of prosperity in agriculture

Farmers benefited only marginally from this revival. The price of foodstuffs was allowed to rise more than farm costs, with the crucial exception of labour. Since production also increased after 1935, farmers' incomes went up by 41 per cent between 1933 to 1938. This was a modest increase when compared with the 116 per cent rise for trade and industry, but substantial compared with that of industrial workers (25 per cent). However, the attempt to reform landholding met with limited success in the face of landowner opposition.

## Case against

There were limitations to the regime's achievements.

## Source 3

*...Under the lash of the dictatorship, the level of economic activity has been greatly increased. The exploitation of labour has been increased; female employment has been increased despite the totally contradictory Nazi ideal of womanhood; and a large number of the* Mittelständlern *(self-employed people) have been transformed into wage-labourers despite the totally contradictory Nazi ideal of their status...*

*But even Nazi trees cannot grow up to the sky. It is true... each year 12–13 billion RM are squeezed from the national income for rearmament ... But one cannot do everything at once with the extorted billions... to increase armaments for the land and air forces* ad infinitum, *to build up a massive battle fleet, to fortify new extended borders, to build gigantic installations for the production of ersatz (synthetic) materials, to construct megalomaniacal grandiose buildings... one can do either one or the other or a bit of everything, but not everything at the same time and in unlimited dimensions...*

*Comments by an SPD analyst, July 1938; quoted in J. Noakes and G. Pridham (eds)* ***Nazism 1919 to 1945, A Documentary Reader****, vol. 2 (1984)*

### For the worker

Despite Hitler's claims to success in the 'battle for work', it was achieved without any change in the actual inequality of the workers. A detailed research into the living standards of factory workers shows that only skilled workers benefited. In contrast, road-building workers not only had pay levels lower than under welfare, but lived in barracks and were subjected to a harsh work discipline so that there was a high turnover. In the late 1930s a great many were employed on airfields and were paid the lowest rates. The number of workers leaving school at 16 increased and larger numbers of women between 1936 and 1939 entered employment especially in electrical engineering on armament orders.

In the late 1930s surveys by the League of Nations on comparative standards of living showed that those in Germany were lower than Britain by a third and than America by a half. Compared with the years 1928–33, many certainly gained by being in work, but this was achieved without any accompanying rise in their standards of living. Even so, for many the years 1935 to 1942 appeared quiet and 'normal'. The claim that 'full employment was Hitler's sole gift to the masses' might be an over-statement, but it remains true that workers worked long hours, under primitive conditions and for low wages. There were no substantial increases in material benefits. By 1938 levels of food consumption had only increased marginally from those in the crisis year (1932), even though the price of foodstuffs was strictly controlled after 1935.

Life was only marginally better in 1933–9 compared with 1931–2. To combat inflation, Hitler sought to control wages and direct labour so that workers who left their job in breach of contract were threatened with temporary loss of the work books which were vital for employment. Wage levels were set in key industries, so that by 1939 wages had fallen by a quarter to a third of the 1932 level and were only marginally higher than they had been in 1928 (see Table 9). The rearmament boom which produced fierce competition for scarce labour and raw materials between the capital goods and consumer-based sector of the economy benefited some groups of workers. Competition led to the 'poaching' of workers and offers of wage increases in defiance of the regime's attempts to contain wage increases to control inflation.

**Table 9** Real wages in Germany, 1932–8

| | 1928 | 1932 | 1934 | 1936 | 1938 |
|---|---|---|---|---|---|
| Real wages (1913/14 = 100) | 110 | 120 | 116 | 112 | 112 |
| Real earnings (1925/9 = 100) | 106 | 91 | 88 | 93 | 101 |
| Wages as a % of national income | 62% | 64% | 62% | 59% | 57% |
| Private consumption as a % of national income | 71% | 83% | 76% | 64% | 59% |

Adapted from R. J. Overy, *The Nazi Economic Recovery 1932–8* (Macmillan, 1982)

Certain groups of workers suffered more than others. Those who were employed in the consumer-based industries suffered most as State spending shifted the emphasis of growth from consumer industries to other major sectors of the economy. After 1936 the amount spent on rearmament for a peacetime economy was high and this required restructuring of the economy for waging war and a restraining of consumer expenditure. The idea of a planned economy in which the interests of all social groups were subordinated to the overriding aim of rearmament – 'guns before butter' – led to a fall in private consumption as a percentage of national income (64 per cent in 1936 falling to 59 per cent by 1938). This was well below that of Britain and the USA.

### For the farmer

Those employed on the land shared this deterioration in condition. The Reich Food Estate had its failures, it was over-regulated and expensive to administer. It was highly unpopular, causing peasant resentment, for it worked to the disadvantage of livestock farmers. They had to rely on imported fodder while prices, particularly of industrial goods, moved against agriculture. There was a rise in agricultural debt, especially on the smaller farms. The regulations of the Reich Food Estate encouraged growing reliance on barter and the black marketeering of illegally retained produce or the slaughter of livestock, especially after 1939. Dependence on fats remained for attempts to grow substitute oilseed plants were uneconomic and of marginal significance.

Those employed on the land were faced with a heavier workload, combined with an increase in duties. There was a flight from the land and the shortage in labour had to be met by using foreign labour and compulsory labour service. This was not enough, so the regime also had to rely on women who worked 75 to 100 hours a week.

### For business people

Small businesses did not benefit as much as did heavy industry, especially in consumer goods where the absence of a consumer boom worked to their disadvantage. Consumer industries were discriminated against with investment and contracts, so performance by late 1938 was lower than in the 1920s. Many small-scale business people who had voted Nazi became disillusioned, although the general benefits of the 1930s blunted resentment. Many closed up and moved to the armament sector in the late 1930s, attracted by the prospect of secure jobs and high pay. Those who were not prepared to cooperate with the regime sold up and went to Switzerland.

A critical shortage of foreign exchange meant difficulty in exporting enough finished industrial goods to pay for vital raw materials and foodstuffs. There was a need to increase imports of goods and raw materials. By the middle of 1934 the foreign exchange position had become critical. Schacht's attempts to promote trade and save foreign exchange by signing bilateral trade treaties met with limited success. The fundamental structural weaknesses became apparent in 1936 when matters came to a head with a balance of payments crisis. Schacht believed that a budget deficit and a balance of payments could not be maintained indefinitely. In early 1936 it became clear to him that as the demands of rearmament and consumption increased, the German balance of payments would go deeply into debt. He therefore suggested a reduction in arms expenditure, in order to increase the production of industrial exports to earn foreign exchange. Such a solution was not acceptable to the army or Nazi leadership and Schacht's influence declined, leading to his resignation and replacement by Walter Funk.

It has been claimed, by some historians, that Schacht only papered over the cracks, for agriculture and industry competed for foreign exchange, while between 1936 and 1937 there was an 80 per cent increase in armament spending. However, Schacht could not resolve the competing demands for scarce resources, so Göring was given increased powers. Hitler would not be persuaded of the necessity to scale down rearmament. Increased power was given to the massive chemicals firm I. G. Farben Trust from 1936 onwards as a result of their experimentation in synthetic chemicals, rubber, petrol, oil and textiles. The company persuaded the government to increase its investment on the promise that it could help Germany achieve economic self-sufficiency. In return, the company made increasing financial contributions to the party and accepted top Nazis on its board of directors.

Economic self-sufficiency was not achieved by 1939 as the shortfalls in the targets of the second Four Year Plan indicate (Table 10). However, these strains were not sufficient to create, as some historians have argued, a crisis in 1939 which persuaded Hitler to go to war.

**Table 10** German production increases in the sphere of the second Four Year Plan

| Commodity | 1936 output | Output in 1936 as a % of 1940 plan target | 1938 output | Output in 1938 as a % of 1940 plan target | Plan target |
|---|---|---|---|---|---|
| Mineral oil* | 1,790 | 12.9% | 2,340 | 16.9% | 13,830 |
| Aluminium | 98 | 35.9% | 166 | 60.8% | 273 |
| Buna rubber | 0.6 | 0.6% | 5 | 4.2% | 120 |
| Nitrogen | 770 | 74% | 914 | 87.9% | 1,040 |
| Explosives | 18 | 8.1% | 45 | 20.2% | 223 |
| Steel | 19,216 | 80.1% | 22,656 | 94.4% | 24,000 |
| Iron ore | 2,255 | 40.6% | 3,360 | 60.5% | 5,549 |
| Brown coal | 161,382 | 67.1% | 194,985 | 81.1% | 240,500 |
| Hard coal | 158,400 | 74.4% | 186,186 | 87.4% | 213,000 |

* including synthetic petrol

From J. Noakes and G. Pridham (eds), ***Nazism, 1919-45, A Documentary Reader*** (1984)

# TASKS

## Sources

Most source questions test your understanding of the material you are given. In the case of the German economy the evidence is statistical and it is important that you practise handling this type of source. Statistics are a useful tool for comparing the performance of the economy both before and during the Nazi regime. However, care has to be taken over the selection of years for comparison. A distorted result is possible if you compare a good with a bad year. Methods of calculating statistics on the German economy have been subject to reassessment over the years, as more sophisticated data sampling techniques and/or new sources of information have emerged. This has led to a revision of interpretations, such as whether the regime was planning for a limited or total war and the degree of preparedness for war by 1939. These different sets of statistics provide an important comment on issues associated both with the generation of new work and with the writing of history.

## What type of questions are asked?

- The first question is usually based on an understanding of the text (**comprehension**). You might be asked to explain the meaning of a phrase or, as in the case of question 1 on page 91, the implications of statistics. The emphasis is on the source material as evidence.
- Look at question 2 and the first part of question 4. These ask you to use two sources to come to a conclusion. You are comparing and contrasting, but the 'to what extent' tests the skill of **evaluation**: you have to decide the relative importance of factors.
- Look at question 3. This requires you to use four statistical sources to come to a conclusion. The 'on what grounds' requires you to rely on comprehension. But 'for what reasons' tests the skill of **analysis**. Most of what you need for this question is in the sources, though you should also make your own judgement.
- Questions 7 and 9 ask you 'in what ways' the statistics 'help to explain or support'. You will need to show your understanding of the statistics, but the word 'help' suggests that your answer should be linked to your wider knowledge and understanding. This is testing the skills of **source utility and historical judgement**.
- Question 8 asks you to consider the 'value' of the Secret Memo. This

involves a discussion of the origins of the memo – its **provenance** – who wrote it? when? to whom? for what purpose? was he present at the event? Questions which ask you to **evaluate** can mean a number of things, *e.g.* you might be asked to distinguish between fact, opinion, judgement. Or you might be asked to recognise deficiencies in the material: its gaps, inconsistencies or limitations. You might be asked to assess the usefulness of a source.

The Secret Memo is valuable: as an insight into Hitler's war aims; as evidence that he was planning for war from 1936; as evidence of Hitler's views on the economy and its relationship to political and rearmament objectives; as an account of Nazi rearmament objectives in 1936. In other words, its value is as a serious statement of intent to wage a war. However, the limitations of the source are that it is not possible to say what kind of war Hitler was planning, or the extent of Germany's war preparedness in 1939.

## Questions

**You will need to consult sources 2 and 3 and tables 3–10.**

**1** Using the evidence of table 5, explain what is meant by the claim that Germany's economic recovery was 'state-led'.

**2** Using the evidence of tables 8 and 9, to what extent can it be claimed that 'economic recovery was achieved at a cost to the workers'?

**3** Using the evidence of tables 6, 7, 10 and your own knowledge, on what grounds, and for what reasons, might it be claimed that 'not all business men benefited from recovery of the economy'?

**4** To what extent, and for what reasons, might it be claimed – on the evidence of tables 3 to 10 – that 'the economic fabric of the country stretched and sagged'.

**5** Read source 2 'The Secret Memo'. Examine the reasons why autarky was such an important priority for Hitler in 1936.

**6** Read source 3 – the comments of the SPD analyst – and study table 10. In what ways do these two sources help to explain the relative failure of the Four Year Plan, by 1940, to achieve its economic objectives.

**7** What is the value to a modern historian of the Secret Memo which launched the Four Year Plan?

**8** How might the regime's statistical evidence be used to support the view that 'Nazi economic policies up to 1938 were partially successful'?

## CHAPTER FIVE

# DID HITLER SUCCEED IN HIS AIM OF CREATING A *VÖLKSGEMEINSCHAFT*?

## Objectives

- To understand the nature of 'community' ideology in the Nazi thinking and in propaganda
- To understand the extent to which this ideology was translated into practice.

**1933**

**April** National Boycott of German shops and businesses
Civil Service Law removes Jews and non-Germans
**May** Trade Unions dissolved and replaced by the German Workers' Front (*Deutsch Arbeitsfront*, DAF)
**June** Marriage Loan scheme for eligible racial applicants
Law to Reduce Unemployment
**July** Law for Prevention of Hereditarily Diseased Offspring
**September** Work begins on autobahns
Reich Entailed Farm Law
**December** Reich Food Estate

**1934**

**January** Law for the Ordering of National Labour – industrial relations were weighted heavily against the workforce and in favour of management
**September** New Plan to control imports
**October** Winter Relief scheme

**1935**

**June** Law for compulsory labour service
**September** Nuremberg Laws (Reich Citizenship Act) and beginning of wide-ranging discriminatory measures against the Jews. Jews not allowed to marry German nationals

**1936**

**September** Second Four Year Plan
**December** Hitler Youth becomes a state youth organisation, with a membership of over 5 million by the end of the year

**1938**

**April** Employment of Jews in business concerns is terminated by the law against 'camouflage of Jewish business undertakings'
**July** Jewish doctors banned from practising
**August** Synagogue in Nuremberg demolished
Jews compelled to add to existing names the forename Sarah or Israel
**September** Jewish lawyers banned from practising
Jews have to carry identity cards
**October** All Jewish passports had to be stamped with 'J'

**November** *Kristallnacht* ('Night of Broken Glass') pogrom throughout Germany, leads to the wild destruction and looting of 7,500 Jewish shops, homes and synagogues
Expulsion of all Jewish pupils from schools, cinemas, universities, theatres and sport facilities
**December** Compulsory closure and sale of all Jewish businesses to Aryans.
Decree for the Struggle against the Gypsy Plague
**1939** **August** Wartime economy measures begin in Germany
Euthanasia programme to kill mentally and physically handicapped patients

# Role of 'the national community' in ideology and propaganda

As you read in chapter 3, Hitler's ideology aimed to restructure German society to incorporate only the 'pure' elements within the community (*gemeinschaft*). Membership of this people's community was open only to 'pure' Germans. Hitler talked of a new social order, a *völksgemeinschaft* ('people's community') which was a romanticised and anti-urbanised image. Literally translated, *völk* means people and *gemeinschaft* a tightly bound and united rural community. Before their seizure of power, the Nazis had made much in their propaganda campaigns of reversing the trend towards urban living to a society based on the peasantry through a policy of 'blood and soil'. The Nazi ideology viewed the peasantry as racially the purest element of the *völk* and as representatives of those traditional values which had become lost in urban society. The Nazi regime stressed that the future Germany 'can only be a peasant state' and Hitler spoke of his vision of establishing a *völkisch* state 'south of the Ukraine'.

*Völksgemeinschaft* was based on the idea that everybody had some claim to equality by virtue of being German. Frequent reference was made in Hitler's ideology of a classless society, which would be at the heart of his people's community. Belonging to such a community would become more important than belonging to a particular class, religion, ideology or region. Hitler aimed to create a national solidarity behind the new regime, to overcome all differences and to create an awareness of ethnic and political unity and the duties this entailed. The members of the national community, the national comrades (*völkgenossen*), were expected to be submissive and loyal and active in the organisations of the regime. The community would 'bind together one nation, one people, one Empire and one Leader'. Hitler was the saviour of this new community while social policy, the basis of the *völk*, was made attractive to all social groups.

A social 'revolution' was 'implied' in propaganda though, as we shall see, it was not directly achieved through policies, for here again there were contradictions and inconsistencies. Nazi propaganda aimed to create the illusion of a 'brave new world'. Various images were adopted to mould public opinion to end the class divisions and conflicts of previous years and achieve a change in attitudes. Propaganda was directed at promoting the new Germany with such slogans as *Ein Reich, ein Völk, ein Führer* ('one country, one people, one leader') and 'this hand rules the Reich, follow it'. Various appeals were made.

### To the peasantry

The peasantry were frequent subjects of the regime's 'High Art' which showed, in a good light, everyday life using ordinary people. The peasant was presented as the backbone of the German community with an emphasis on traditional themes, such as the peasant sower scattering the seeds by hand and using horses rather than tractors. Traditional values were restored. Paintings which showed a ploughing peasant protected by the soldier with women working in the background conveyed the image of a people working together in the new people's community. The recurring image was of a nation working the land, with the military figure representing protection. The peasant family and old age were idealised in public (though in private, euthanasia was carried on). Propaganda aimed at getting people back to the land though, as we shall see later, this attempt at social engineering failed.

### To the workforce

The workforce was promised work, and improved wages and conditions in an attempt to win over those industrial workers who had not really voted Nazi. Campaigns were launched by Goebbels and by the German Labour Front which had replaced the trade unions.

The 'Battle for Work' was a labour-intensive, government-sponsored public works scheme responsible for such projects as the building of autobahns (motorways). The German Labour Front developed a leisure section which regimented the leisure activities of the low paid.

**Figure 12** Nazi propaganda poster by Ludwig Holwein: *Dein KdF WAGEN (Völkswagen)*

The 'Strength through Joy' campaigns prescribed the correct methods, time and content of leisure for the sole purpose of increasing worker productivity. Campaigns such as 'You too can travel' were organised and subsidised cruises at a time when few workers had experienced this before the Nazis came to power. Holidays were highly organised on the holiday-camp model. Luxury hotels were 'opened up'. It was leisure policies such as these which gave the illusion that the Nazi regime was achieving a 'social revolution'. There was also the people's car, the *völkswagen* (see Figure 12) – a 'strength through joy' car. Starting in 1936, workers paid 5 marks a week, stamped in a book, to save for the car – though none had been delivered by 1939 when war broke out. The scheme was both remarkable and resourceful for it made an important contribution to economic recovery and helped deal with the problem of inflation. It was a clever means of forced savings, or rather indirect taxation, for the money was never repaid.

Finally, the 'Beauty of Work' campaign was a sub-section of the 'Strength through' Joy organisation. Again it was masterminded by Goebbels. It sought to improve status and working conditions as a substitute for wage increases. It launched a number of campaigns to publicise good working practices, such as 'fight against noise', 'good ventilation in the workplace' and 'clean people in a clean plant'. These were designed to encourage employers to improve working conditions and much was made of the number of factory inspections which had led to improved conditions. Posters showed the transformation of houses and improved standards at work. New housing estates were built as part of its campaign to improve conditions in factories and provide model houses and community projects on model estates.

### To women

Women figured prominently in the 'High Art' of the regime. They were presented in various images – either in a classical pose or within the family. A woman's half-naked figure was used to represent 'a time of ripeness'. One image was of a family listening around a radio because Hitler was keen that people should hear propaganda. To this end a cheap radio was produced, the *völksempfanger* (people's receiver). Goebbels used the radio to emphasise Germany's cultural heritage.

### To the family

The family was always presented as a peasant family with three children or more. There was a certain inconsistency because Germany was overpopulated, but propaganda always encouraged the family to increase its size. The solution to overpopulation would be provision of settlements for colonies. Racial purity was also emphasised in the images of the family; young men were six feet (1.8 metres) tall, blond and blue-eyed; girls were peasant looking to suggest they would be good mothers.

### Appeal to youth

One propaganda message was 'this hand rules the Reich, follow it' which used the face of a young blond boy with an idealistic expression looking upwards, which represented the future. Other images carried the message 'youth serves the Leader'. All other youth organisations for those between the ages of 3 and 18 were banned in favour of the Hitler Youth organisations which were used to collect money for a range of Nazi organisations.

### To the Jews

Propaganda also concentrated on the Jews and always carried the same message: 'the Jews are our misfortune'. The regime sought to build up hatred, especially among young children. Frequent use was made of pictures showing Jews leaving Germany – then all would be 'sweetness and light'.

# The Regime's success in creating a *völksgemeinschaft*

## A 'pure' community

Hitler's drive to achieve a *völksgemeinschaft* of Aryans of a healthy physical and mental condition proved to be the most consistent, coherent and revolutionary aspect of Nazism. In its determination to achieve racial purity the regime succeeded in eliminating those 'impure' people it considered to be a threat. This policy was accelerated during the Second World War. Following the success of the German army in conquering large parts of Eastern Europe, Himmler was made Reichskommissar for racial matters with responsibility for strengthening the German race. The 'New Order', which sought to implement Hitler's *völkisch* state 'south of the Ukraine', led to the resettlement and extermination of those races considered to be 'impure'. In so doing it produced a different society both in Germany and in its conquered territories; but one based on social destruction.

## Non-Aryans, such as Jews and gypsies

Many textbooks have tended to ignore the plight of Germany's 30,000 gypsy population under the regime. Although they were not seen as such a serious racial threat as the Jews, they were included in the 1935 Nuremberg Law for the Protection of German Blood and Honour which banned marriage and sexual relations between Aryan and non-Aryans. At first the regime contented itself with detaining the gypsies in camps and putting them to work, as well as sterilising them as part of the ethnic cleansing policy. Then, in December 1942, gypsies were sent to Auschwitz, where they were subjected to medical experiments carried out by Dr Mengele. Of the 20,000 transported to Auschwitz, 11,000 were murdered, while the others were transferred elsewhere. Within Eastern Europe thousands of gypsies were murdered by SS extermination units. Within Germany only 5,000 of the original 30,000 gypsies survived the war.

Hitler's policy against the Jews in Germany, who numbered about 500,000, also proceeded by stages.

**1933–5:** during the first two years, the Jews experienced relative freedom from persecution as Hitler and the regime directed its efforts to consolidate its position and bring down unemployment. Thus during 1934 the regime confined its anti-semitic policies to prohibiting Jews from the professions. Policy changed during the course of 1935, when Hitler was in a stronger position. Although the SA had been brought under control after the purge of Röhm, there was a fresh outburst of anti-semitism among the rank-and-file who demanded a 'Jew-free economy'. This Hitler resisted because Jewish firms were still important for economic recovery, but he did surrender to the propaganda contained in Julius Streicher's *Der Stürmer* which demanded restrictions on sexual contact between Jews and Gentiles. To this end he passed the Nuremberg Race Laws in September. These banned marriage between Jews and German citizens and deprived Jews of voting rights. Hitler met with no resistance from his civil servants who viewed the legalising of anti-semitism as a defence against further disorder on the streets.

**1935–9:** despite this increase in hostility the Jews, up to the end of 1937, succeeded in keeping control of their businesses and could still use most of the amenities open to other Germans. Signs of a more radical policy appeared in the winter of 1937–8. As the German economy moved into rapid expansion, the big industrial concerns, eager to get rid of their Jewish competitors, pressed the regime to proceed with the 'Aryanisation' of the economy. Göring, plenipotentiary for the Four Year Plan, reduced their raw materials allocation and they ceased to receive public contracts after the spring of 1938. Following the *Anschluss* with Austria in March 1938, Göring ordered Jews to register all property over 5,000 marks in value and they were prohibited from selling without permission. The employment of Jews in business concerns was terminated by the law against 'camouflage of Jewish business undertakings', while Jewish doctors, dentists and lawyers were forbidden to offer their services to Aryans. The climax to this increasing radicalisation came on 9 November in the event known as *Kristallnacht* ('Crystal Night'). The assassination of Ernst von Rath, a diplomatic official at the German embassy in Paris by a Jew, two days earlier gave the regime the opportunity to launch its first state-led persecution of its Jewish community. Jewish shops, homes and synagogues were destroyed, hundreds of Jews were injured or killed and others were sent to concentration camps. After this, the position of Jews deteriorated more rapidly as a number of discriminatory decrees followed. Jewish pupils were expelled from schools, cinemas, universities, theatres and sport facilities. In many cities, where the bulk of the Jewish population lived, Jews were banned from entering designated Aryan areas. This legislation was carried out by local fanatics, so that by the time of the outbreak of war the Jew had been isolated within German society.

This radicalisation of the regime's anti-semitic policy on the eve of war was not due solely to Hitler's influence but can also be explained by political developments, which might seem to give weight to the arguments of those who incline to a structuralist interpretation of decision-making. During the course of 1937–8 power shifted to the more radical elements in the Nazi Party as the pace of foreign policy increased (refer to Part One). Hitler's dismissal of those conservative elites who had worked with the regime led to a significant change in the balance of power. Economics Minister, Schacht, who had always been aware of the international repercussions of a policy of 'Aryanisation', resigned leaving Göring in supreme command of the economy. He was determined to create a 'Jew-free' economy as quickly as possible and Hitler agreed to Göring's suggestion that the time had come for a properly coordinated and centrally directed policy. This opened the way for an intensification of the policy of persecution and Göring was put in charge, to the benefit of the large industrialists.

During the spring of 1939 Hitler made a number of hostile comments relating to his determination to destroy the Jews which have been interpreted by 'intentionalist' historians as confirmation that Hitler had a long-term aim to get rid of the Jews. This view is not shared by others who have pointed to the apparent inconsistencies and contradictions in Nazi policy against the Jews. They argue that the Nazis had no clear idea where they were going in their anti-semitism. They point to Himmler's encouragement of an emigration policy since 1934 which suggested that Hitler did not have an unwavering commitment to Jewish extermination. Himmler's emigration policy met with limited success. Only 120,000 of Germany's 503,000 Jews had left by

1937 and many had subsequently returned. The annexation of Austria in March 1938, with 190,000 Jews, intensified the emigration policy. In the course of 1939, 78,000 Jews were forced out of Germany and 30,000 out of Bohemia and Moravia. The climax to this policy came in the summer of 1940 with the 'Madagascar Plan' to transport four million Jews from West Europe to the island. The plan, which had been popular in the 1920s, had the support of Himmler and Hitler approved a draft plan. It only failed because Britain refused to allow free access by sea.

**1939–45:** the outbreak of war opened up a new and more intense persecution of Jews. Expansion brought far more Jews under Nazi control and presented the regime with the major task of dealing with them. In Poland, Jews were rounded up and put into ghettos, but this created problems of food and accommodation. It was at this stage that the outlines of a new 'solution' of the 'Jewish question' were taking form. Hitler informed close associates of his plans to remodel Eastern Europe on racial lines, turning their peoples into slaves serving a master race of German settlers.

It is at this point in the chronology of Nazi anti-semitic policies that historians have diverged in their interpretations.

- **Intentionalists** (*e.g.* Eberhard Jackel and Andreas Hillgrüber) argue that Hitler decided on the Final Solution sometime in the summer of 1941 in the belief that a Russian collapse was imminent and that the opportunity had arrived to achieve his lifetime ambition. Whether he gave a specific order, or merely a 'prompting initiative', is an open question. No written order has been found though that is not unusual given Hitler's method of working.
- **Structuralists** (*e.g.* Martin Broszat and Hans Mommsen) argue that the decision was made only in late autumn of 1941. Hitler is accepted as exercising considerable influence on the course of events, but he is seen as not always the initiator. They argue that the Holocaust was not planned by Hitler but developed out of a deteriorating situation not anticipated by the Nazis though probably made inevitable by the mounting radicalism of their anti-semitism.

On what many historians consider rather weak evidence, structuralists argue that the Final Solution was preceded by a policy to resettle European Jewry east of the Urals and that failure to defeat Russia wrecked the plan. Even so, Hitler in October 1941 ordered the transportation of Jews to the eastern territories to begin. Because there was no way over the Urals they congregated in the ghettos of Eastern Poland until resources were strained to breaking-point and epidemics started to break out. The response of local SS was to begin, on their own initiative, to murder Jews either by gassing or shooting, but there was the problem of getting rid of the bodies. Sometime in October or November, Himmler was supposed to have informed Hitler of these events and he approved the extension of these practices to include the whole of European Jewry. It is even possible that the initiative was taken, not by Hitler, but by Himmler.

What is the significance of this debate? Behind this disagreement over what might seem a relatively minor question of timing lie fundamental differences over Hitler's role and control over decision-making in the Third Reich and particularly his role in connection with the 'Holocaust'. On 31 July 1941 Göring ordered Heydrich to complete the task he had given him in January 1939 'to bring about a complete solution of the Jewish question within the German sphere of influence in Europe' and to prepare a plan for the 'Final Solution' of the Jewish question. This directive was referred to by Himmler at the Wannsee Conference where the details of the Holocaust were worked out. All frontiers were closed to Jews and plans were started to kill 11 million Jews in Europe. Initial arrangements seem to have been haphazard and makeshift but this was typical of the Third Reich. The evidence of Adolf Eichmann and Rudolf Höss, commandant of Auschwitz, suggests that throughout the summer and autumn of 1941 the SS worked on this new project. Restrictions placed on Polish Jews were extended to German Jews. This was followed in the autumn by the transportation of Jews to the camps.

What is the present state of the debate? Historians now argue that when Hitler spoke to Himmler in October/November 1941 he merely approved an existing extermination plan. The chaos in Eastern Poland in the autumn and the local shootings and gassings were not because a resettlement plan – which the structuralists argue existed – had failed, but because an impatient Hitler ordered deportations from Germany to begin before the extermination facilities had been completed. This would seem to support the intentionalist claim that Hitler kept Goebbels and Rosenberg ignorant of his real intentions. When he spoke of resettlement he really meant extermination and he left others to push the plan along. What is not in doubt is the meeting of various government and Party agencies with top SS officials, under the directions of Heydrich, in January 1942 at a Conference at Wannsee, which agreed to final details of the Holocaust. The word 'extermination' was not mentioned, but the intention was clear: Jews were to be worked to death or gassed. During the spring extermination camps were set up at Auschwitz, Chelmno, Majdanek and Treblinka. For the next two years vast numbers of Europe's Jews were transported eastwards to the death camps where a policy of extermination was carried out. Between 1942 and autumn 1944, when Himmler ordered its suspension, it has been estimated that some 5 to 6.5 million died in the camps.

### Public reaction to the persecution of the Jews

Hitler made use of the anti-semitic traditions in Germany, though no German could have conceived of the extent to which Hitler would go to achieve racial purity. People, in general, were largely indifferent to the Jewish question, but eventually the volume of anti-Jewish propaganda had its effect and people came to approve of the aims of the Nazis' anti-Jewish policy. During the war people chose to ignore the stories about the atrocities in the occupied countries. There were rumours about extermination, but the systematic gassing programme in the camps appears, according to Ian Kershaw, to have been largely unknown. The last two years of the war saw even less public interest despite an increase in hostile propaganda, perhaps because the removal of so many had made them seem irrelevant.

### The mentally and physically handicapped

These were affected by the regime's eugenics policy to purify the population of its weak elements. This started with the 1933 Sterilisation Law and was subsequently extended by its euthanasia programme of 1939. Heredity courts were set up but evidence of being workshy or a communist often led to a sterilisation decision. From 1934 to 1945 between 320,000 and 350,000 were sterilised. These included prostitutes, alcoholics and those suffering from diseases such as Parkinsons. The regime claimed that once sterilised an individual would be restored to full status as 'national comrades' though, given the emphasis on fertility, this was not true. Many people supported the idea of sterilisation. Fears of a deterioration of the race in the next generation had been increased by progress in medical science which meant that more people with hereditary defects were surviving into reproductive adulthood. It was also fashionable to blame many social ills – such as alcoholism, pauperism, prostitution and criminality – on heredity. Eugenics was seen as a way of getting rid of the dregs of society.

Euthanasia was directed against those who had incurable and/or severe handicaps and injuries. Between 1939 and 1941, when the programme existed officially, 72,000 died. Public hostility to the programme led to its abandonment, though it continued secretly in concentration camps. Between 1941 and 1943, another 30,000 to 50,000 people were gassed in the camps on grounds of mental illness, physical incapacity or simply racial origin (either Jew or gypsy).

### The socially inefficient

Tramps and beggars – some 300,000 to 500,000, many of whom were young homeless unemployed – were organised into a mobile labour force to do compulsory work in return for their board and lodge. Disorderly persons were sent to preventive detention and sterilised. With an increasing shortage of labour after 1936 the regime sent some 10,000 workshy to concentration camps where experiments were carried out, often on the young, for purposes of social-biological selection. This policy appeared to be popular with many Germans and was welcomed by local authorities as a means of getting rid of problem people. It was only defeat in 1945 that ended plans to extend this policy of compulsory sterilisation and probable eventual death through hard labour in concentration camp conditions.

## A united community based on social conformity

Many Germans, and foreign observers, were impressed by what appeared to be a transformation in people's attitudes. The regime introduced a number of policies to strengthen people's belief that they belonged to a new national community. As part of the drive to achieve social conformity, the term *völkgenossen* ('national comrades') was adopted. Everyone was expected to attend the parades and speeches which became a feature of the new public rituals which celebrated events in the Nazi calendar. Germans were required to show the national community at work. A number of welfare measures were introduced to give people an opportunity to present a vivid expression of the *völksgemeinschaft* at work and proof of their loyalty to the regime. Hitler emphasised the importance of individual and collective responsibility of the people as opposed to that of the State. At the basis of this responsibility was the door to door 'collecting of money' and food.

**Welfare policies and their success**

***Winterhilfe* Scheme:** the Winter Relief fund, introduced in 1933, was intended to help the unemployed millions. It operated from October to March and each year was inaugurated in a wave of publicity. For the dedicated Nazis, it became a test of political faith for the masses. Even after full employment had been achieved by 1936, the system continued, but became a massive ritual aimed at raising popular feeling and encouraging self-sacrifice. Failure to give Winter help and/or not enough was condemned so that what was presented as a voluntary charity became a compulsory tax which ate into workers' wages, making some of them in turn liable to receive relief. By 1937/8, when unemployment had been solved, 8.9 million received relief under this scheme.

**The *Eintopf* ('One pot') meal:** propaganda posters referred to the *Eintopf* (One-Dish-Sunday) as the 'meal of sacrifice for the Reich'.

**Cult of motherhood:** the regime attempted to make 'motherhood' an attractive financial proposition through a series of grants and interest-free loans to newly married couples and tax relief schemes provided the wives withdrew from the labour market. It was also concerned to increase population which was encouraged in a number of ways. Anti-abortion laws were enforced and contraceptive advice and facilities were restricted. Family allowances were improved (10 marks a month were given for the third as well as the fourth child and 20 marks for the fifth). Couples who had larger families were given additional rewards, such as a child subsidy given to those on limited incomes. It was a lump sum to be spent on furniture and clothing. A quarter of the marriage loan was converted to an outright gift on the birth of each of the first four children. Fertile mothers were awarded the Honour Cross on 12 August (Hitler's mother's birthday) each year – bronze for 4 and more children, silver for more than 6 and gold for 8. Mothers received preferential rations and safer air-raid shelters in the war when mother worship peaked.

Domestic assistance was given to mothers by means of the duty-free year for girls and during the war foreign labour was allocated to agriculture. Marriages were arranged and divorce encouraged among childless couples; medical inspections identified 'racially inferior stock' along with a programme of compulsory sterilisation.

Statistics on marriage and birth rates suggest that these policies were not successful. They show that from a low point in 1933 the birth rate increased, reaching a peak in 1939 and thereafter it slowly declined again. The problem for historians is to decide whether Nazi population policy produced this rise or whether other social, economic and even personal psychological reasons were responsible. In the main historians have argued that the policies, representing Hitler's social engineering on behalf of the people's community, were not responsible for the rise in the birth rate. It was more likely to be the result of the end to depression and a younger age of marriage, such as occurred in other countries.

Nazi views on women were irreconcilable with the realities of twentieth-century trends which saw the emancipation of women. They were also irreconcilable with Nazi objectives of rearmament and military conquest. Consequently, Nazi policy towards women and the family was contradictory, confused and ultimately a failure. The divorce rate climbed steadily, juvenile delinquency increased from 16,000 in 1933 to 21,000 in 1940. Family relationships were undermined as a result of quarrels over the treatment of barren wives; conflicts increased between generations, especially mother and son, over such issues as premarital sex and maternity cases. By 1945, 23 per cent of all young Germans had venereal disease and prostitution had quadrupled. Ultimately, women were not confined to the home, despite the initial appearance of success when Nazi policy coincided with the withdrawal of female labour because of the slump. This was particularly true of non-professional and academic women. However, the regime could make little headway against the growing trend of young adult women in the consumer goods industry and the necessity to employ women because of the growing labour shortage.

Apart from its programme of social welfare, the regime understood the importance of organising the people and of controlling not only their work, but also leisure. Clubs and private associations were put under party dominance and all aspects of life were organised.

The reaction of people to life in the people's community is difficult to assess. Under the impact of press censorship and the institutionalisation of terror, an independent public opinion did not exist. The image of German society conveyed in the newsreels and press was always one of mass enthusiasm and commitment. It is clear that the regime operated on a remarkable degree of consent and social conformity.

Central to this was the positive image of Hitler as the Führer accompanied by concrete successes, such as full employment and restoration of Germany's position as a world power. To a certain extent everyone, apart from those considered to be racially impure, benefited from the regime especially in terms of the economic revival.

Moreover, a very large section of the German people shared the basic attitudes of Nazism, such as nationalism and militarism, as well as hostility to unpopular minorities. They also supported the firm line taken to overcome unemployment and discourage deviant groups such as homosexuals, tramps, criminals and the workshy.

It is equally true that people sought escape by becoming inward-looking and retreating into the home and family. They were aware of the danger of criticising the regime.

Even so, dissent and unrest existed among both the peasantry and the industrial workers, although this did not express itself in open opposition. The regime's opponents were weak due to ignorance, lack of political will and the fear produced by its coercive powers.

## A peasant-based national community

The regime failed in its aim to create a community based on a stable class of landholding peasants. A number of policies were introduced to help the peasantry – such as the Reich Food Estate which controlled prices and granted subsidies, and the Reich Entailed Farm Law which provided for land ownership. Some farm ownerships were created between 1933 and 1936 and peasants were also settled in Eastern Europe, Poland and Posen. Historians have differed in their interpretation of these policies. Some have seen in these tentative policies indication of a social revolution because it defied social trends elsewhere, but there is no agreement on this. However, the 1933 inheritance laws and resettlement had occurred before the time of the Nazis and resettlement did not proceed far under the Nazis. Others have seen the policy towards the peasantry as a front to get them to work harder and provide more food to link up with autarky.

Schemes of rural resettlement were bound to fail because they conflicted both with Hitler's expansionist plans and with the long-term trend of a rural drift to the towns. The realities of the politics of the Third Reich – namely Hitler's need to retain the support of the elites, whose interests were threatened by Nazi support of the peasantry – led Hitler to choose the Junkers. The peasantry were sacrificed, so that not only was there no substantial change in their position, it was in fact worse in 1939 than it had been in 1932.

By 1939 there was a:

- flight from the land as labour shortages meant that peasants worked harder, especially in 1939 and 1944 when food quotas were raised as part of the war effort. They had a lower standard of living and suffered from disease;
- 20 per cent drop in productivity and public opinion reports showed the negative reaction to the regime;
- need to find additional sources for recruitment of agricultural labour, such as youth, prisoners, slave workers and women. Employment of eastern labour and prisoners-of-war during the war years aroused fears for the safety of farmers' wives and property, such as occurred in 1944 when slave labourers rioted.

Far from becoming the backbone of society, the peasants found that not only had there been no change in their class position, but their economic status had deteriorated.

## A classless society

Hitler claimed by 1937 that he had succeeded in breaking down the old class system with all its prejudices and had achieved a genuine people's community. This claim has been hotly debated by historians. Part of the historical debate stems from the nature and limitation of the evidence:

- Historians have to adopt the tools of the sociologist to arrive at an understanding of social hierarchy with its elements of class, status, social mobility and social revolution. This raises the problem of definition for such terms and concepts can be vague and are influenced by an individual's perspective and politics.
- Social science disappeared in Germany after 1933 and this makes historical reconstruction difficult though not impossible. Statistics continued to be published, newspapers and periodicals were informative and many problems affecting agriculture and industrial labour were discussed in public.
- Central to the debate is an analysis of people's attitudes and patterns of response to the regime and this requires a different kind of source base, one which includes 'history from below'. Major advances in the availability of such evidence on the experience of different social groups only became available in the 1960s and even more so since the 1970s when there was a growth of interest in the 'history of everyday life'. One such source, a *Life History and Social Culture in the Ruhr 1930–1960* edited by Lutz Niethammer, was published in 1983. It was based on the findings of a large oral history project carried out by the universities of Essen and Hagen.

> Its findings indicate that people had very positive memories of the 1930s as a time of peaceful private advance, secure employment and well-ordered family life. Many had positive memories of a guaranteed pay packet, preferential treatment for large families and the availability of new sport and leisure activities, such as visits to the theatre, and package holidays either to distant places in Germany or abroad. The 1940s were recalled as a time when many saw an increase in qualifications and mobility which shattered the old social environment for good. It also saw greater hopes of improvement among manual workers and lower level white-collar workers which continued into the 1950s.

Obviously there are major difficulties in interpreting such sources given the image of terror, mass murder and war associated with National Socialism.

In spite of these problems of interpretation, the most recent writings on the Third Reich reject the view that the existing class structure was altered. Those historians who are critical of the view that society was restructured have described the changes between 1933 and 1939 as a 'revolution of form not substance', stemming from Hitler's concern to 'deceive' the people. They have argued against the previously held view of the 1960s that class consciousness changed, apart from a greater awareness of 'class consciousness' and 'status'. They believe that subjective attitudes towards the regime continued to be influenced by people who did not feel themselves to be part of the German 'people's community'. Hitler's new social order contained in *völksgemeinschaft* was, in many respects, merely a propaganda gimmick. In reality, deep social divisions and sources of serious discontent remained scarcely concealed by the propaganda image and were countered by severe repression.

If a social revolution was achieved it came as a result of the elimination of people; Jews, those elites implicated in the plot to assassinate Hitler in July 1944, priests and mentally/physically handicapped in the euthanasia programme – which produced a different society. The strongest argument for a revolution is based on the regime's social destruction. Social change was provoked by war but this was not intentional.

The impact of the regime on different social groups can be summarised as shown in Table 11.

**Table 11** Impact of the regime on different social groups

| Group | Main features of the impact |
|---|---|
| Workers | As you read in chapter 4, despite Hitler's success in achieving an economic recovery and full employment, there was no change in their actual inequality. They continued to play a traditional role as workers. Propaganda campaigns – such as 'strength through joy' and 'beauty of work' – did not win them over to National Socialism for many saw the destruction of the trade union organisation as antagonistic to the aims and interests of the working class. |
| Middle class | Were also disillusioned and felt that their interests had been 'betrayed' as a result of rearmament. Election promises to protect small businesses against the large department stores were ignored. Moreover, between 1942 and 1943 shops and workshops were closed down because they were not necessary to the war effort. |
| Elites | Safeguarded from attack by Hitler's purge of the left wing of his Party in June 1934, they continued to prosper and be dominant. The great landed estates of the Prussian Junkers were not carved up, big business continued to benefit from the regime's economic policies, while the High Command of the army remained in the hands of the aristocracy. Prussian militarism and its social basis, the Junker aristocracy, ended with the collapse of the Third Reich. |

## TASKS

**Individual or group activity**

The organising theme of this activity is the 'Myth and reality of the Third Reich'. Working either on your own, or in a study group, and using either pen and paper or a computer, consider the following concepts of völksgemeinschaft:

- membership open only to 'pure' Germans
- a society based on the peasantry
- a völkisch state south of the Ukraine
- a classless society
- national solidarity
- a submissive and loyal people
- one leader

In each case, look at the role each played in:

- ideology
- propaganda image
- policies
- effect/impact/change.

Use the information contained in this chapter and the notes you have made from your reading of the preceding chapters.

Prepare a summary of your findings for presentation to the whole group. Use either a flipchart or an overhead projector.

## CHAPTER SIX

# DID HITLER PLAN FOR TOTAL WAR?

## Objectives

- To understand that historians can hold different opinions about the past which can lead to differing interpretations of war in the Third Reich
- To understand the extent to which Hitler's war plans were translated into practice.

## Historians' views on the economy and war preparations

Much debate has centred on German levels of armaments in the 1930s and the extent to which the economy was fully mobilised for war in 1939. The disagreement among historians about what kind of war Hitler was planning is partly explained by the varying statistical analyses of the German economy since the early 1950s. Statistics on rearmament are unreliable; during the 1930s the Nazis always inflated the size of their armed forces, especially planes, for propaganda purposes. Also, it is difficult to isolate armament expenditure from other investment. This is certainly the case with the issue of mefo bills and the building of the autobahns. The former were a means of raising money to finance the recovery of heavy industry. It is difficult to say what proportion of the mefo bill issue was for arms purposes, though one source claims as much as 50 per cent in the mid 1930s. Hitler's autobahns were part of his 'Battle for Work' campaign, but they also had a military significance in their capacity to move large numbers of men and materials quickly by road. Historians have not agreed whether they should include them in rearmament.

As a result of these attribution problems, a number of interpretations on the nature of Germany's war effort have appeared over the years. Until the 1980s it was argued that:

1 Hitler decided to gamble on small forces to fight opportunistic wars (*Blitzkrieg*) in order to avoid strains on the population.

2 The economy operated on a 'peace-like' war basis throughout

1939–41 and only changed when Speer became Minister of Armaments in 1942, while a full-scale commitment was not fully realised until 1944.

**3** There was a clear gap between Hitler's ambitions and economic and military policy.

Historians' views on rearmament and war preparation prior to the 1980s can be summarised as follows:

**Three historians and a summary of their interpretation**

**A. J. P. Taylor, *The Origins of the Second World War* (1964)**
Hitler was not really planning for war in 1939. The proof of this lay in the level of German rearmament which by 1939 was by no means great enough to sustain a European, let alone a world, war.

Few of the statistics available since the 1960s support Taylor's opportunist view. The limited character of German rearmament which proves that he did not want a war, is only supported by the early figures published in the late 1950s. These were compiled when the study of the German economy under the Third Reich was still in its infancy and source material was unsatisfactory.

**T. W. Mason, *Some Origins of the Second World War* (1964)**
Hitler was forced to go to war to divert attention away from inherent structural tensions and economic crises which first appeared in 1937. Mason's structuralist perspective of the regime was that the economic policies adopted by Hitler created a long-term crisis, apparent from 1936, from which there was no easy way out. Mason argues that the crisis facing Germany in 1939 was acute labour shortages, inadequate exports and a generally overheated economy. To continue rearmament Hitler had to find new sources of raw materials, food and labour. Hitler went to war to escape from structural tensions and crises produced by rearmament and dictatorship. According to Mason: from March 1933 to March 1939 the Third Reich spent about half as much again on rearmaments as Britain, though of course Germany was starting from a much lower base level.

- At no time was anything like the full capacity of the German economy devoted to war production.

- Hitler was planning to employ *Blitzkrieg* (lightning war) tactics, rather than long campaigns of trench warfare. German armaments were not sufficient in 1939 to sustain a long war.

*These are both from E. M. Robertson (ed.)* ***The Origins of the Second World War*** *(Macmillan, 1971)*

**B. E. Carrol, *Design for Total War: Arms and Economics in the Third Reich* (Mouton, 1968)**

The title is misleading in that the author does not agree that the Nazis planned a total war. Her conclusions are that from:

- 1934 Germany moved towards a war-orientated economy;
- 1936 the economy was dominated by arms;
- 1938 it was a war economy;
- 1942 it was a total-war economy with 50 per cent or more economic resources devoted to war purposes.

Although German investment in military hardware was not overwhelming before 1939, arms production up to 1939 was equal to the combined commitment of the USA, Britain and the USSR.

Recent research, using improved and more sophisticated data sampling techniques has challenged this interpretation.

**R. J. Overy, *War and the German Economy: A Re-interpretation* (1982)**

Overy argues that the *Blitzkrieg* theory does not fit the facts. Hitler planned for a total war, though well after 1939, and when war broke out Germany mobilised as fast as it could. Things went wrong when economic planning got out of phase with foreign policy. He supports this argument by citing:

- Hitler's speeches about the long drawn out conflict;
- economic planning which was all long term;
- Hitler's plan was for a war in the mid 1940s or later;
- the sheer size of Nazi rearmament in the late 1930s was much bigger than was needed for *Blitzkrieg*. War coming in 1939 threw the long-term plans into confusion showing up unsolved structural problems in the Nazi economy.

## The present state of the debate

The current state of the debate suggests that:

- The foundation for a full economic mobilisation was laid before 1939, in the 'disguised' rearmament of 1933–6. This was followed by the direct move to gear the economy for total war associated with the Four Year Plan (1936–9). According to the evidence of General Thomas, head of the armed forces economic staff and in constant touch with the war machine, Germany was totally mobilised for a full war by July 1941.
- These arrangements provided for rearmament in depth (factory capacity, machinery, raw materials, labour) as well as width (stockpile of armaments), and for the fullest possible use of civilian resources in wartime. Registers of labour ensured a speedy recruitment of men and women for the war industries.
- Emphasis was also put on the psychological preparation of the people to persuade them to accept the cuts in living standards.

In 1939, although these preparations were still incomplete, Germany was devoting 32.2 per cent of its national income to war; compared with Britain's 15 per cent – a differential which continued throughout the war (as Table 12 shows).

**Table 12** Select statistics on the German and British war effort (1939–44)

| a Percentage of war expenditure in total national income | 1939 | 1940 | 1941 | 1942 | 1943 | 1944 |
|---|---|---|---|---|---|---|
| Germany | 32.3 | 48.8 | 56.0 | 65.6 | 71.3 | – |
| Britain | 15.0 | 43.0 | 52.0 | 52.0 | 55.0 | 54.0 |
| **b Percentage of women in the total of civil employment** | **1939** | **1940** | **1941** | **1942** | **1943** | **1944** |
| Germany | 37.3 | 41.4 | 42.6 | 46.0 | 48.8 | 51.0 |
| Britain | 26.4 | 29.8 | 33.2 | 34.8 | 36.4 | 36.2 |

R. J. Overy '"Blitzkriegswirtschaft"? Finanzpolitik, Lebensstandard und Arbeitseinsatz in Deutschland 1939–42' ***Vierteljahrshefte für Zeitgeschichte***, vol. 36 (1988)(translated by Edgar Feuchtwanger)

# Impact of Hitler's war plans on the economy

## 1939–41

By the summer of 1941 Hitler's armed forces had achieved considerable military successes (you might want to refer to the timeline in Part One for details). These not only won Hitler and the regime valuable popular support, but also conveniently disguised such economic problems as the shortage of raw materials, the need to ration food from September 1939 and the general inefficiency of the bureaucracy coordinating military and economic policies. Although the image of Germany was one of order and efficiency, British economic mobilisation for war was much quicker in the years 1939–41. In spite of all the talk of total war, Germany failed to match the output of economies less well-endowed with resources and skilled labour.

By 1941 a number of weaknesses had emerged:

- **The economy was overstretched.** A crisis was provoked in 1941 with the failure to meet the production needs set in the Göring Plan to quadruple the size of the air force. The plan revealed the weaknesses which rendered management of the war economy ineffective. These ranged from the absence of sufficient men, combined with bottlenecks and poor planning in the machine tool industry, to serious shortages in transport provision. A similar problem was faced by the navy when it attempted to expand.
- **There was a general lack of planning.** The military believed they should take control. They smothered the economy with regulations and restricted industry, insisted on high-quality weapons and discouraged mass production. They satisfied short-term military requirements.
- **Germany had failed to exploit the areas** it had conquered effectively. It was this failure to produce enough weapons from the continent-wide resources at its disposal which led early researchers to argue that Germany was not really preparing for total war.
- The real problem confronting Germany was the **premature outbreak of war**. Enormous difficulties were faced in trying to

wage the big war before all the programmes that would support it had been completed. Much of the early part of the war was spent in indecision between trying to complete the great targets set in the Four Year Plan and switching to the mass production of weapons. The economy was pulled in both directions with the result that neither was met satisfactorily.

- There was also **great inefficiency and wastefulness** brought about by competition between the armed forces, poor central control of the economy and military demands for excessively high-quality weapons. This was apparent in the aircraft industry. It doubled its resources, but achieved only a 10 per cent increase in production between 1939 and 1941, rising to 20 per cent in 1941.

## 1941–2

It was the failure to provide enough aircraft to invade Russia in 1941 which eventually led Hitler to intervene and take a more direct interest. In May 1941, he held a high-level conference which identified the problem as one of efficiency and rationalisation. A series of comprehensive decrees were issued which aimed to end the crisis in war production.

- The turning-point came in December 1941 with the Rationalisation Decree. This ordered that the war economy should be simplified and streamlined in order to mass produce. This reorganisation ended the confused planning, poor coordination and wasteful duplication of the earlier years. Within two years, the productivity of the workers in the armaments sector almost trebled.

- The December decree also ordered a restructuring of the control of industry. Up to the end of 1941 the responsibility for actually running the war economy on a day-to-day basis had been in the hands of competing administrative empires; the one under the Four Year Plan and the other under the armed forces. Hitler was critical of both and blamed them for the muddle. He decided to take the economy more closely under his general supervision and to put civilians in control. The death, in February 1942, of his first Minister of Armaments, Fritz Todt, gave him the opportunity to appoint Albert Speer.

## Speer's policies, 1942–5

Speer recognised that it was the failure to get direct backing from Hitler which had limited the efforts to mobilise the economy before 1942. Speer used the Führer's authority to push through his economic programme, though he was not always successful – as in the case of his failure to overrule objections and officially conscript women. Speer had a different war to fight from that of his predecessors in terms of scope, scale and intensity. He was concerned to expand arms production in 1943–4 against the background of increasingly devastating allied bombing of Germany. Speer showed brilliant technical and organisational ability, but he clashed with fellow high-ranking Nazis over the source of the labour required to continue with war production. Ideological considerations meant that Speer lost his attempts, both to employ more women and to treat camp labour more humanely.

Speer introduced a number of policies.

**1** He encouraged a policy of industrial self-responsibility. The controls and restraints previously placed on business, in order to subject it to Nazi wishes, were relaxed. In their place was established a Central Planning Board which had a number of committees, each one representing one vital sector of the economy. This Board ended the bureaucratic agencies which had competed against each other. In this way, Speer maintained overall control of the economy.

**2** He also appreciated that businessmen had been left out of most decision-making. Although they did what the authorities told them to do, they made no effort to correct inefficiency or incompetence. Speer sought to overcome the negative attitude of industry by allowing industrialists a considerable degree of freedom and by breaking the power of the armed forces over production and the training of labour.

### Success?

These policies had some success. Between 1942 and 1944 weapon output trebled, but the resources allocated only increased from 10 to 15 per cent. This was achieved through greater efficiency, savings across the war economy in capital and labour and the increasing employment of foreign labour.

### Limits on the success of this policy

This was due to strategic bombing which placed a ceiling on Germany's efforts. There has been a great deal of research in Germany on this which has led to a change in views of the effects of bombing.

- It has always been argued that allied bombing had marginal effects on economic performance, but historians need to look at the statistics for specific, preselected bombing targets. By 1944, according to a report sent to Speer, there was a decline in output of aircraft (by 31 per cent), military vehicles (40 per cent) and tanks (35 per cent). The decline was in current programmes and it might have led to Germany receiving half the output expected. This undermined Germany as a military force in 1944–5.
- Allied bombing by 1943 diverted roughly two million men and 50,000 artillery pieces. A third of all production of German heavy guns and radar electrical equipment was also diverted to dealing with allied bombing. Added to this was the colossal effort required to move operations underground. All this represented a diversion of resources away from production of weapons.

So it is surprising that the German economy performed as well as it did by 1944. However, such economic successes as were achieved could not reverse the declining military situation. By the end of 1944 Allied forces were advancing from both east and west and the German war economy degenerated rapidly. The breakdown of communications, the shortage of vital raw materials and a lack of labour meant that the war could not be continued effectively.

## Source

*If war had been postponed until 1943–5, as Hitler had hoped, then Germany would have been much better prepared. It would also have had rockets, jet aircraft, intercontinental bombers, even possibly atomic bombs. Though Britain and France did not know it, declaring war in 1939 prevented Germany from becoming the superpower that Hitler wanted. The commitment to full mobilisation had been there from the start, but, as Hitler complained, 'mismanaged'. The drive for total war became* blitzkrieg *by default'.*

*R. J. Overy '"Blitzkriegswirtschaft"? Finanzpolitik, Lebensstandard und Arbeitseinsatz in Deutschland 1939–42'* ***Vierteljahrshefte für Zeitgeschichte*** *(1988)*

# Impact of Hitler's war plans on the people

## As consumers

Hitler's concern that the people should not be deprived of a basic minimum of food consumption failed. From the start, the German people did not have an easy war. Wartime taxation increased rapidly and consumer spending was restricted. Unlike Britain, where rationing was introduced more gradually and for certain foodstuffs only, Germany introduced a comprehensive rationing from the first weeks of the war. There was a 25 per cent decline in consumption per head between 1939 and 1941, compared with Britain's 12 per cent. The reduction accelerated as war progressed. Some food became unavailable and the people found themselves restricted to a monotonous diet of black rye bread, potatoes and vegetables. The cutback in consumption rapidly created shortages of essential clothing for labourers and of other essential civilian equipment which was diverted to meet the demands of the armed forces. Propaganda encouraged people to save and the level of savings rose by 50 per cent by 1941 compared with 1939. Although Germans did not starve during the war, life became strenuous and demanding, particularly for women.

## As labour

A planned direction of labour was introduced to draft it into the armed forces or move it to war work and, where possible, to train the unskilled and women. A register of labour was compiled, along with a comprehensive set of guidelines on labour allocation, so that the armed forces and industry would be clear about what kind of labour they were entitled to. The Ministry of Labour published regular checklists of labour shortages for agents to know what kind of labour was required. Labour was also subjected to multiple shift working as part of the strategy to increase industrial capacity. Between 1939 and 1940 plans were put into action to convert factories previously devoted to car and furniture consumer production to war production of aircraft and armaments. Increased investment also occurred in capital-intensive industries such as iron, steel, chemicals and synthetic oil, at the expense of consumer production. The shortage of workers for the arms industries, mainly skilled metalworkers, was met by a special priority rating to protect firms from loss through conscription.

The pattern of labour distribution reflected the needs of the war. Heavy industry and metalworking expanded their labour supply, whereas building and consumer industries contracted up to 1941. The pattern of distribution changed very little between 1941–3, showing no change in the middle of the war. The greatest change came in 1939 and early 1942, reflecting how many of these workers were working on orders for the armed forces. In 1941 the services took 40 per cent of textiles output and 44 per cent of all clothing which left much less capacity for civilian needs than output figures suggest (see Table 13).

**Table 13** German industrial labour forces working on orders for the Armed Forces, 1939–43 (per cent)

| | 1939 | 1940 | 1941 | 1942 | 1943 |
|---|---|---|---|---|---|
| All industry | 21.9 | 50.2 | 54.5 | 56.1 | 61.0 |
| Raw materials | 21.0 | 58.2 | 63.2 | 59.9 | 67.9 |
| Metal manufacture | 28.6 | 62.3 | 68.8 | 70.4 | 72.1 |
| Construction | 30.2 | 57.5 | 52.2 | 45.2 | 46.7 |
| Consumer goods | 12.2 | 26.2 | 27.8 | 31.7 | 37.0 |
| Index (1939 = 100) | 100 | 229 | 248 | 256 | 278 |

From R. J. Overy, 'Mobilisation for Total War in Germany, 1939 to 1941', ***English Historical Review***, vol. 103 (July 1988)

## Employment of women

Overy now rejects as myth the Nazi propaganda claim that Germany would not mobilise women for war work. In fact, the proportion of women in Germany who worked was exceptionally high in 1939. This was due partly to the demands of a fully-employed rearming economy and partly to the movement of male workers from agriculture. More and more women were left to do the work on the land and there was a growing labour shortage.

**Table 14** Percentage of women in the total of civil employment

| | 1939 | 1940 | 1941 | 1942 | 1943 | 1944 |
|---|---|---|---|---|---|---|
| Germany | 37.3 | 41.4 | 42.6 | 46.0 | 48.8 | 51.0 |
| Britain | 26.4 | 29.8 | 33.2 | 34.8 | 36.4 | 36.2 |

Taken from R. J. Overy, '"Blitzkriegswirtschaft"? Finanzpolitik, Lebensstandard und Arbeitseinsatz in Deutschland 1939–42' ***Vierteljahrshefte für Zeitgeschichte***, vol. 36 (1988)

Table 14 shows that by 1939 women already constituted a much larger part of the workforce in Germany than in Britain. This differential was maintained. Women were also forced to work harder to make up for shortfalls in the male workforce. There was a substantial redistribution of women away from consumer to war and war-related industries, working on orders for uniforms and military equipment of all kinds. Women moved rapidly in 1940–1 into heavy industries and manufactures serving the war effort. They worked long hours with little help until more foreign labour was brought in to keep agriculture going in the middle of the war. The bulk of the German workforce, both male and female, was mobilised for war work between 1939 and the beginning of 1942; thereafter the shortfall in labour demand had to be met from other sources. During the 1942–4 period occupied Europe provided labour to make up the losses to the armed forces and in fighting. It was against this background of declining living conditions and long hours that the victimisation and brutality shown towards foreign forced labour occurred.

## Employment of foreign labour

At the end of 1944 over eight million foreigners were working in Germany. The employment of such vast numbers was one of the most distinctive features of mobilisation for war. The great majority were industrial or agricultural workers. Their legal status within the Nazi New Order was defined by their place of origin. So Russian workers were herded into trucks and housed in a fortified camp, while the French could look for their own lodgings. The first full-time workers began to leave from France and Belgium in September 1940 because of heavy unemployment and wage controls within their own country. They were recruited by agencies set up by the Reich Labour Front and were employed on the same terms as German workers.

Foreign labour was also recruited from Germany's conquered territories:

- Poland played a key role in providing workers for this New Order. From the beginning of 1940, Hans Frank, the Nazi governor-general of Poland, was ordered to recruit one million workers, three-quarters of them for agriculture. Even though compulsion had to be used from May 1940, it was not until the autumn of 1942 that the one million level was achieved.

- The failure of the German army in Russia changed the character and scope of the war, and of the foreign labour contingent. Foreigners were needed in their millions to expand productivity, especially in the munitions factories. Fritz Sauckel, who was responsible for finding this extra labour, persuaded Hitler to relax his racial and political objections to the employment of Russians. Between March 1942 and December 1942 Sauckel recruited over 2.6 million mostly from Russia and Eastern Europe and thereafter around 340,000 arrived per month, resulting in 6 million by 1945. Such a number changed the composition of foreign workers in Germany and their legal status. The Russians were always the largest single group of foreign workers after 1942 and accounted for half of the female foreign workers. Hitler's original idea had been that Russian women would be employed as domestic servants to relieve German women. However, their capacity for industrial work led to their use in this field, where they became the most disciplined and most productive of the foreign workers. They were employed in the aircraft and other industries geared to the war effort.

The new workers were regarded with loathing so that German law insisted on great distinctions between the eastern workers and the others. The former were confined to one of the special camps built to house foreign workers. The sanitary arrangements were appalling, and with poor medical attention and poor rations, the death rate was high.

- Between 1942 and 1943 Sauckel pressured the French government into compelling its industrial workers to move to Germany. This culminated in the Labour Laws of February 1943 which conscripted young workers for compulsory labour. Although these French workers had the reputation for careless work and sabotage, their skills made them indispensable. They were joined by workers from Holland and Italy.

Speer favoured a system of setting foreigners to work on German contracts in their own country. He introduced such a system in June 1943, but it met with little success. In 1943 Sauckel's efforts began to fail as numbers from Russia and France started to fall; men preferred to join the resistance than leave for Germany. The result was that Germany could not use their labour even in their country of origin and Sauckel's policy was discredited. However, he refused to change his views and even in 1944 a further million foreign workers were added.

## Final defeat of Hitler's war aims

During the first years of the Second World War, allied air attacks on Germany met with little success because of the small size of Britain's Bomber Command, its inadequate equipment and defective technique, combined with a deliberate policy not to bomb civilian areas. This had changed by May 1942 when a thousand bombers were launched against Cologne. By August 1943 about 40,000 German civilians were killed in a series of raids against Hamburg. Even so, by the winter of 1943–4, the heavy bombers of Britain and America had not achieved a reduction in essential war production, nor did they prevent the German armed forces from continuing in Russia and Italy. This was to change during 1944 when the Allies acquired a mastery of the air over Germany. This made possible a series of devastating attacks, which had a disastrous effect on Germany's war economy and on the population. Both these factors were to lead to Germany's defeat.

The German people were left isolated and demoralised. Absenteeism increased during 1944/5 when it was 25 per cent on any day of the year at the height of the bombing. This can partly be explained by illness and the evacuation of some eight million. This social dislocation caused not only local labour shortages, but also local disturbances which had a severe effect on the functioning of the war economy. The regime had to rely on terror which reached its highest point in 1945 when it was directed against the German people. The total number of concentration camp prisoners in Germany reflected the growth of extremism within the regime. The figure for the 1930s could be considered moderate, the rise by 1942 represented the imprisonment of suspected opponents in occupied countries, while the large figure by 1945 was due to the forced labour scheme for armament production (see Table 15). By this time there were 20 main and 165 subsidiary camps.

**Table 15** Total number of Germans held in concentration camps in Germany

| | |
|---|---|
| 1934–8 | 7,000–10,000 |
| 1942 | 100,000 |
| 1944–5 | 500,000 |

In February 1945 greater casualties were caused by the devastating raids on Dresden. Bombs killed 400,000 civilians and destroyed many towns and the great German synthetic oil plants which were ruined beyond repair. Oil became unobtainable and the communications system was reduced to the point where administration began to break down. National resistance broke down and Berlin fell on 2 May 1945.

# Tasks

## Individual or group activity

Below are two hypotheses representative of the debate on Hitler's war planning. Read through this chapter and select the information and evidence you would use in support of each. Is one hypothesis sounder than the other?

**Hypothesis A**
Hitler was planning to employ *Blitzkrieg* or lightning war tactics, rather than preparing for long campaigns of trench warfare. German armaments were not sufficient in 1939 to sustain a long war.

**Hypothesis B**
Hitler planned for a total war, though well after 1939 and when war broke out Germany mobilised as fast as it could.

You should decide on how you are going to present your argument.

# FURTHER READING


**Chapter 1**

G. Layton *Germany: The Third Reich, 1933–1945*, Hodder and Stoughton (1992)

S. Taylor *Germany 1918–1933*, Duckworth (1986)

W. Carr *A History of Germany 1815–1945*, Arnold (1979)

John Hiden *The Weimar Republic*, Addison Wesley Longman (1974)

M. Kater *The Nazi Party: A Social Profile of Members and Leaders 1919–1945*, Blackwell (1983)

**Chapter 2**

Martin Broszat *The Hitler State*, Addison Wesley Longman (1981)

Alan Bullock *Hitler: A Study in Tyranny*, Penguin (1975)

J. C. Fest *Hitler*, Penguin (1977)

J. C. Fest *The Face of the Third Reich*, Penguin (1972)

D. Geary *Hitler and Nazism*, Routledge (1993)

K. Hildebrand *The Third Reich*, Allen and Unwin (1984)

Ian Kershaw *The Nazi Dictatorship, Problems and Perspectives* (3rd edition), Arnold (1993)

Ian Kershaw *The 'Hitler Myth': Image and Reality in the Third Reich*, Oxford University Press (1987)

Ian Kershaw *Hitler*, Addison Wesley Longman (1991)

R. J. Overy *Göring the Iron Man*, Routledge (1984)

Albert Speer *Inside the Third Reich*, Warner (1993)

Hugh Trevor-Roper *The Last Days of Hitler*, Papermac (1987)

**Chapter 3**

Adolf Hitler *Mein Kampf*, translater: Ralph Mannheim, 1939, Hurst and Blackett (ed.), Hutchinson (1969)

Alan Bullock *The Third Reich*, Weidenfeld and Nicolson (1955) – chapter 8

Alan Bullock *Hitler, A Study in Tyranny*, Penguin (1961) – pages 36–46 and 397–408

W. Shirer *The Rise and Fall of the Third Reich*, Pan (1964) – chapter 4, pages 108–148

R. G. L. Waite *Hitler and Nazi Germany*, Holt, Rinehart and Winston (1965, 1969) – pages 59–64 and 93–115

## Chapter 4

R. J. Overy *The Nazi Economic Recovery 1932–8*, Macmillan (1982)

J. Noakes and G. Pridham (eds) *A Documentary Reader: Nazism 1919–45*, University of Exeter Press (1984) – vol. 2, pages 259–300

H. A. Turner *German Big Business and the Rise of Hitler*, Oxford (1985)

H. A. Turner (ed.) *Nazism and The Third Reich*, New York (1972)

D. G. Williamson *The Third Reich*, Addison Wesley Longman (1982) – pages 26–32

*Articles:*

W. Carr, 'The Determinants of German Foreign Policy 1933–9', *History Sixth* (October 1988)

R. J. Overy, 'Hitler and the Third Reich', *Modern History Review* (November 1989)

## Chapter 5

R. Bessell *Life in the Third Reich*, Oxford (1987)

R. Grunberger *Social History of the Third Reich*, Penguin (1974)

D. J. K. Peukert *Inside the Third Reich, Conformity and Opposition in Everyday Life*, New Haven, London (1987)

## Chapter 6

Douglas Botting *In the Ruins of the Reich*, Allen and Unwin (1985)

J. Noakes and G. Pridham (eds), *A Documentary Reader: Nazism 1919–45*, Vol. 3 'Foreign Policy, War and Racial Extermination', University of Exeter Press (1988)

Albert Speer *Inside the Third Reich*, Weidenfield and Nicolson (1970)

*Articles*

R. J. Overy, 'Hitler's War and the German Economy, A Re-interpretation', *Economic History Review* (1982)

R. J. Overy, 'German Domestic Crisis and War in 1939', *Past and Present* (August 1987)

R. J. Overy, 'Mobilisation for Total War in Germany 1939–41, *EHR* vol. 103 (July 1988)

# INDEX

## KEY TERMS



## PROFILES



## MAIN INDEX